D1195367

brown bagging it:

THE LUNCH BOX
IDEA BOOK

ADELINE GARNER SHELL
KAY REYNOLDS

 Sovereign Books • New York

Published by Sovereign Books
A Simon & Schuster Division of
Gulf & Western Corporation
Simon & Schuster Building
1230 Avenue of the Americas
New York, New York 10020

Designed by Libra Graphics, Inc.
Manufactured in the United States of America
10 9 8 7 6 5 4 3 2 1

Library of Congress Cataloging in Publication Data
Shell, Adeline Garner.
    Brown bagging it.

    Includes index.
    1. Luncheons. I. Reynolds, Kay, 1911-   joint
author. II. Title. III. Title: Lunch box idea book.
TX735.S44   641.5'3   78-10945
ISBN 0-671-18414-8
ISBN 0-671-18342-7 paper

contents

brown bagging it:

**THE LUNCH BOX
IDEA BOOK**_____

introduction_____

Once upon a time, taking your lunch was considered corny, odd, a little on the cheap side unless you were a forest ranger, a dam builder, or worked at construction or in a factory where there were no restaurants. But now, a complete turnaround! It's the "in" thing to take lunch. What did it? Terrible restaurants. Service with a snarl instead of a smile. Long lines. Long waits. Then, gobbling. Indigestion. Out-of-sight prices. Fast-food chains, where it's impossible to get a balanced meal, and if you want one in a restaurant, it's too expensive.

That's what led to the Great Rebellion. The rebels took to the lunch box—or should we say—took the lunch box, and they're taking it everywhere—offices, factories, trucks. You see lunch toters high in the air on building girders, down in the ground in utility repairs, in tunnels, in parks, elegant building plazas in big cities, on ten-foot-long desks in sumptuous executive suites, and next to sewing machines in clothing factories. You also see lots of lunch boxes at the beach, at roadside tables, and along riverbanks.

Millions have discovered that a meal from home is a meal to enjoy. You eat what you like. It's fresh and good. It's no hassle at lunchtime. It's restful and refreshing. The rules for good, enjoyable lunch box meals are simple. Pack variety. Pack good nutrition. See the "Is It Enough Nutrition?" Checklist, page 116. And the happy ending to the lunch box rebellion is that you save a mint of money! One friend saved enough in a year taking her lunch to her place of work to buy a round trip charter air ticket to Europe. We've made it simple to select, organize, pack lunch and maintain your tote equipment.

The "Mini-Catalog of Lunch Box Equipment," page 119, bring you up to date on the wide selection of accessories available for lunch box toting. Different styles of vacuum bottles, thermo jars, lunch boxes, thermo insulated bags, plastic containers of many varieties and uses, are covered in this catalog along with cleaning and caring for each piece of equipment.

The "Sanitation and Health" checklist, page 117, is a guide to good food storage, preparation, packing and carrying practices that help avoid the digestive distress or food poisoning that can occur with careless handling. This is particularly important in hot weather.

If it's so good and it saves so much money, why doesn't everybody take lunch? For a lot of reasons. People fall into the "same old thing syndrome." They take the same old thing every day and end up hating it. In this book you'll find dozens of different things to take for lunch. Practical. Good tasting. Nutritious.

People say they hate sandwiches, so why take lunch? Who said it has to be a sandwich? We give ideas and recipes for salad totes, gourmet goodies, hot dishes, elegant soup meals, and even Scotch Eggs (page 100).

True, the sandwich is the linchpin of the lunch box. But even those who like them complain that sandwiches carried from home arrive soggy, mangled, bland, and battered. This need never be. "Perfect pack" sandwiches are easy to do. Here are snappy sandwiches for toting that bear no resemblance to cardboard on arrival.

Another big groan from lunch box toters concerns time. They never seem to have enough of it in the morning to pack lunch. This is a pure-and-simple matter of organization, especially when packing sandwiches. We give the management solution to schlepping sandwiches —all the details—streamlined, easy, foolproof. Just for starters, why make the sandwich completely at home? Wrap the ingredients, toss them into the lunch box, and you're off! Assemble same at point of eating. If that seems too radical, there are lots of made-from-scratch sandwiches to tote, too.

Another problem is a serious one, the plight of people on low-calorie diets. Don't worry. There are tote foods for reducers in chapter 7, and they're delicious. No austerity.

So let's begin.

1 sandwich_____
is
king

Sandwiches are the lunch box standard, so we'll deal with them first, bearing in mind that there are many other ways to pack a lunch box, most of them more interesting than sandwiches.

Two slices of cardboard white bread nuzzling bologna or processed cheese is a dull way to make a sandwich. The possibilities are endless and include a lot of happy ideas for sandwich fillings.

Those who say they don't have enough time to pack a sandwich in the morning will find they do if they follow our management tips—the executive way to pack a sandwich.

How about that discouraging soggy sandwich? See "How to Take the Sog Out of the Sandwich" below and suffer no more when the lunch box is unpacked.

Complete sandwich menus are given because most sandwiches need crunchy accompaniments to provide pleasure and texture contrast, and to add the nutrition needed to round out a tote meal.

HOW TO TAKE THE SOG OUT OF THE SANDWICH

NO-SOG SANDWICHES. The best way is not to put the sog *in* the sandwich in the first place. Just take the makings—the bread, a spread such as butter or mayonnaise, a filling such as tuna salad or sliced roast beef, and the crispy parts such as salad greens or shredded carrot

7

or celery. Pack these separately in plastic containers or a sandwich wrap of your choice. Tote them in a lunch box, insulated lunch bag, or brown paper bag. Make up the sandwich at work, just before eating.

THE WAXED PAPER PLOY. Instead of using a spread on the bread, place on top of the bread a piece of waxed paper cut slightly larger than the bread. Place half the salad greens to be used in the sandwich on top of the waxed paper. Place the filling on the greens and top with the remaining salad greens and a second piece of waxed paper. Top that with bread, but do not cut the sandwich. Pack either in a plastic sandwich container or waxed paper, plastic sandwich bag, plastic wrap, etc. When ready to eat the sandwich, remove waxed paper by gently sliding it out of the sandwich. If desired, carry butter or margarine or mayonnaise separately to put on the bread immediately before eating and then cut the sandwich. If packing a spread seems too much work, add the spread when making the sandwich and add waxed paper as suggested above. Follow these logistics and you will never have a soggy sandwich.

THE SEGREGATION SYSTEM. When making a sliced meat, cheese, or chicken sandwich, place the meat between two slices of buttered bread and wrap. Carry separately the crunchy, moist sandwich makings such as greens, tomato slices, chopped carrot, salad mix, etc., and a spread such as mayonnaise or mustard, and add to the sandwich only when you are ready to eat. This does not work as well with moist fillings such as egg salad, tuna, or salad mixtures.

Insulator Bread Spreads

Another way to avoid soggy sandwiches is to insulate the bread from the filling with a lining of margarine, butter, or peanut butter. The fat content of these spreads prevents the bread from getting soggy.

Mayonnaise, salad dressing, chili sauce, and pickle relish add good flavor and variety to sandwiches, but they do not insulate. They penetrate the bread and make it soggy. It is best to carry them separately.

Make-Ahead Bread Spreads for Extra Flavor

To add zest and variety to sandwiches, make your own flavored bread spreads. These spreads are not a substitute for fillings but they do enhance the flavor of sandwiches as well as provide insulation against sogginess. They're best when made ahead and refrigerated so the flavors have time to blend well. This is a time-saver in the morning or at night when packing sandwiches, and surefire insurance against the boring sandwich.

Make-Ahead Spreads

Combine and mix until well blended:

¼ cup very soft butter or margarine
½ teaspoon lemon juice

Add ONE of the following tastemakers and mix until well blended:

2 teaspoons prepared mustard
½ teaspoon dry mustard
½ teaspoon finely chopped onion
½ teaspoon finely chopped garlic
2 tablespoons chopped fresh parsley
2 tablespoons chopped fresh chives
2 tablespoons chopped fresh watercress
1 teaspoon horseradish
1 tablespoon olive paste
2 teaspoons chili sauce
1 tablespoon chutney
¼ to ½ teaspoon dried herbs such as tarragon, marjoram, dill, or oregano
2 tablespoons grated Parmesan cheese
½ teaspoon paprika
½ teaspoon curry powder
½ teaspoon filé powder combined with
½ teaspoon paprika

Add salt and pepper to taste. Mix well. Cover. Store in refrigerator until ready to use.

VARIATIONS. In place of butter or margarine, use the same amount of sour cream or yogurt. Increase or decrease amounts of ingredients to taste.

SANDWICH TIMESAVERS—
THE EXECUTIVE ATTITUDE

Four ways to save time:

1. Don't make the sandwich at home at all. Pack the parts for assembling at the point of eating, as previously described.

2. Set up a Lunch Box Organizer Center, a shelf and/or drawer which holds:

> Sandwich wraps such as waxed paper, plastic wrap, aluminum foil, sandwich bags, plastic sandwich carriers
>
> Lunch boxes, insulated lunch bags, or brown paper bags
>
> Plastic wraps and waxed paper from bread and other food products such as fresh fruit. Rinse these well before recycling
>
> Ricotta, cottage cheese, or other liquid-tight, leak-proof containers that may be used for carrying greens as well as other foods; baby-food jars for carrying spreads or relishes

—Toter's Own Favorite Bread Spread_____

Flexible spreader such as a spatula for spreading fillings

Sharp knife for cutting sandwiches

Vacuum bottles of all kinds. (Store uncovered to prevent mustiness.)

Plastic containers and lids

Napkins or paper towels

Salt and pepper shakers

The Fisherman and the Earl. While standing near a wharfside lunch place for fishermen in New Jersey, Adeline Shell saw a reenactment of the Earl of Sandwich story. A man about to board a fishing party boat ordered a deli cold cut plate. The boat captain suddenly shouted "Last call" just as the man was about to eat his deli lunch. Just like the Earl of Sandwich, the fisherman took the sliced roll, piled the corned beef, potato salad, cole slaw and pickle on one piece, topped it with the other, and ran for the boat with lunch in hand. Perhaps lunch boxers might like to take the hint and carry a deli combination on bread for handy eating.

3. Set up a Refrigerator Sandwich Lunch Organizer Center that will hold these items, close together, in the refrigerator:

> Butter or margarine
> Mayonnaise
> Sandwich fillings such as meat, cheese, hard-cooked eggs
> Jars or plastic packs of homemade insulator spreads, as previously described
> Relishes such as pickle relish
> Ready-to-eat raw vegetables such as carrot sticks, salad greens, etc.
> Fresh fruits
> Desserts

4. Set up a Freezer Sandwich Lunch Organizer Center that holds:

> Made-ahead sandwiches
> Individual servings of sandwich fillings to slip into bread; these go from freezer to lunch box in an instant. Filling will thaw by time of eating; this method also keeps things cold while they are being toted
> Frozen cookies
> Frozen juice in leakproof, liquid-tight plastic containers to use as lunch box beverages and to keep the rest of the food cold while being toted
> Leakproof, liquid-tight containers filled with water to freeze, or a freeze-gel container, for portable refrigeration

THE SANDWICH HOME ASSEMBLY LINE

When making two or more sandwiches, save time and energy by using mass production techniques. Reserve ample work space to make the job easier.

Here's how it goes:

1. Place bread slices in two rows. As slices come from the loaf, keep them together, one slice placed on top row, and the next slice placed directly beneath it in the lower row. This keeps matching-size slices together. With these slices, the filling stays put, and the sandwich filling and bread do not dry out.

2. Place a dab of butter or margarine on each slice of bread. Spread it to the very edges of the bread to cover the whole slice. Bread that has not been spread clear to the edges will dry out, or if the filling is very wet, the edges of the bread will become soggy.

3. Then place a serving of filling on each slice of bread in one row only. Spread the filling evenly over the slice. Top with the other slice of bread.

4. Cut, and pack in a sandwich wrap, or place in an air-tight plastic sandwich container.

Carry the crunchy part of the sandwich, such as greens, separately.

SPECIAL TIP. It is easier to pack a sandwich uncut. It doesn't dry out, or fall apart, and it can be divided when ready to eat, for utmost freshness.

Any Number Can Play

The above applies to just one person making and packing sandwiches, but the smart sandwich executive organizes the whole family for the sandwich assembly line. The work can be done the night before or in the morning. Once the family falls into the routine, it's all done in a matter of minutes, though it may be chaos the first few times around. Junior might end up with two sandwiches in his lunch box, and Sister none, but this is adjusted quickly. As many as six people can form a sandwich assembly line, or the jobs can be divided among fewer people.

First decide whether it is more efficient to make sandwich fillings and sandwiches in the morning or to make them the night before and refrigerate them. One person can make the sandwich filling and another can make the insulator sandwich spread, if used. In some instances, the same person makes both, depending upon the number of people available for the assembly line.

If the filling is made the night before or early in the morning, another person gets together everything else needed to make the sandwiches. (This is where the Sandwich Lunch Organizer Centers come in handy.) The same person also puts all the things back.

Another person is responsible for making the sandwiches. This includes spreading the butter or insulator on the bread and adding the sandwich filling.

A fifth person is responsible for packing the sandwiches and placing them in the lunch boxes or brown bags. A sixth person is responsible for the salad, for a dressing when used, for the fresh fruit, and for putting these things into the bags.

If a beverage is carried, and beverages differ, it might be wise to let each lunch toter be responsible for his or her own. Otherwise, the job can be assigned to one person.

Sandwich-making steps and packing can be divided according to personpower in your family. Don't hesitate to teach children these jobs. They can do them very well. Smart lunch toters should check out their own bags before leaving to be sure they got some of everything. Mistakes do happen.

If the kitchen is too small for this big an assembly line, simply have two different persons take turns doing the various steps each week.

When making more than one kind of sandwich, such as chicken sandwiches and egg sandwiches, time is saved by completely making one kind of sandwich before starting the next.

TO FREEZE OR NOT TO FREEZE

Unfortunately, most sandwich fillings do not freeze well. Those sandwiches that do, such as sliced chicken, beef, or peanut butter without jelly, should be made of the freshest possible bread and filling ingredients. This ensures good taste and keeping quality. Freezer sandwiches should be eaten within two to three weeks after freezing.

Freezer sandwiches are sometimes soggy when thawed. To avoid this, follow the method given above of spreading each slice of bread to the edges with a coating of butter, margarine, or peanut butter when the taste is appropriate.

Do Not Use Mayonnaise

Mayonnaise, when frozen, breaks down and becomes oily. It should never be used on the bread or in fillings for freezer sandwiches.

To make a spread of cooked meat, fish, or poultry, or a sandwich to be frozen, use butter or margarine or sour cream rather than mayonnaise or salad dressing to bind the ingredients.

Avoid These Ingredients in Freezer Sandwiches

Here are some popular sandwich ingredients, which, alas, do not freeze well:

> Sliced soft cheese
> Cheese spreads
> Cottage cheese
> Most raw vegetables such as salad greens, onion or tomato slices
> Cooked egg *white*
> Liver sausage and liver spreads
> Luncheon meats
> Olives
> Pimiento
> Pickles of all kinds
> Piccalilli
> Chili Sauce
> Jelly, jams, and preserves

Sandwich Ingredients That Freeze Well

> Cooked, sliced, diced or ground meat, fish or poultry
> Cooked egg *yolk*
> Baked beans
> Roquefort or blue cheese
> Peanut butter
> Bread

Fortunately, bread freezes well. To freeze bread for sandwiches, butter two slices of bread. Place buttered sides together. Wrap in moisture-proof material. Label, date, and freeze. When ready to use, just transfer bread directly to lunch box. Carry frozen filling in a separate container and put sandwich together at place of eating. The ingredients will have thawed.

To Pack Freezer Sandwiches

Sandwiches for the freezer should be packed in moisture proof materials such as freezer wrap or heavy plastic wrap.

The "drugstore wrap" is the most efficient way to pack freezer sandwiches because it protects the sandwich and is easy to handle once you learn how. It's done basically the same way as wrapping a gift package.

Drugstore wrap: Tear enough wrap from the roll to go around the sandwich 1½ times. Place sandwich in center of wrap. Bring ends of wrap together over the sandwich. Fold over about ½ inch to ¾ inch and crease along the fold. Press wrap down and against the sandwich at the open end to force out air. Fold ends standing against end of sandwich to form sealing points. Fold ends over, tight against sandwich and seal with freezer tape. On tape, label the type of sandwich and the date packed.

SANDWICHES: THE SUPER SIX

1. THE EGG SALAD SANDWICH

It may surprise some people to discover that, according to surveys, the cold egg sandwich is the most popular lunch box sandwich.

It's even more surprising that many people don't know

how to "boil" an egg. The result is a rubbery disaster with an unpalatable white and a hard yolk that is often discolored. First of all, good hard-cooked eggs are not boiled. The expert way to cook an egg is to bring the water to a boil and immediately take it off the stove. Here are the easy details of cooking a perfect hard "boiled" egg for a perfect egg sandwich.

How to Hard-Cook an Egg to Perfection

Ideal hard-cooked eggs have egg whites that are firm, not rubbery. The yolks are yellow, opaque, not discolored, and the texture is firm and pleasantly mealy.

For perfect hard-cooked eggs, buy eggs five to six days before they are to be used. Store them in the refrigerator. Storage allows the air space at the rounded end of the egg to expand. This makes it easier to peel off the shell after the egg is cooked.

To cook eggs in the shell, have them at room temperature by removing them from refrigerator for about two hours. To hurry the process, cover the eggs with warm, never hot, water for about 20 minutes. Place eggs in an enamel saucepan large enough to hold them without crowding, and allow for adding cold water to at least 1 inch above the tops of the eggs.

To help prevent cracking of eggs during cooking, puncture them first with a sharp needle at the center of the large rounded end. Penetrate only the shell to allow air to escape.

Using high heat, heat the water in which the eggs have been placed only to the point of a full rolling boil. Remove from heat at once and cover the pan with a tight-fitting lid. Allow covered eggs to stand in hot water for 20 minutes. Pour off hot water and cool eggs by running cold water over them. This stops the eggs from cooking and prevents discoloration. It's easier to peel eggs if this is done immediately. If eggs are not to be eaten at once, it is better to store them in the shell. Refrigerate until ready to use or to carry.

Basic Egg Salad Sandwich Filling Plus Variations

3 hard-cooked eggs, cut in large pieces, or chopped into small pieces

½ teaspoon salt

pepper to taste

3 level tablespoons mayonnaise

Place cut-up eggs in small bowl. Season with salt and pepper. Add mayonnaise and mix gently with eggs. Add more mayonnaise, if needed. But, remember—you want a sandwich filling to be moist, not wet and soupy. Makes 2 to 3 sandwiches. VARIATION: Add ¼ cup, or more, chopped celery.

Variations of Basic Egg Salad Filling

1. VARY THE "BINDER." In place of mayonnaise, use salad dressing, yogurt, sour cream, tartar sauce, or a combination of mayonnaise and sour cream or mayonnaise and yogurt.

2. VARY THE SEASONING. Add ¼ teaspoon dry mustard to basic recipe, or to taste.

3. TRY NEW EGG COMBINATIONS. Incidentally, don't overlook the simple, sliced hard-cooked egg sandwich, a great favorite.

4. EGG-OLIVE SANDWICH FILLING. Combine and mix gently 3 cut-up hard-cooked eggs, ¼ cup chopped ripe or stuffed green olives, 2 tablespoons each of sliced celery and chopped carrot, mayonnaise to moisten, and seasonings to taste.

5. EGG-SARDINE SANDWICH FILLING. Combine and mix 3 cut-up hard-cooked eggs, ¼ cup cut-up sardines, 1 tablespoon chopped parsley, mayonnaise to moisten, and salt, pepper, or cayenne to taste.

6. EGG-FRESH VEGETABLE SANDWICH FILLING. Combine and mix 3 cut-up hard-cooked eggs, ¼ cup chopped celery and radishes or tomato, mayonnaise to moisten, and minced chives, salt, and pepper to taste.

7. EGG-HAM SANDWICH FILLING. Combine and

mix 3 cut-up hard-cooked eggs, $\frac{1}{4}$ cup chopped ham, minced onion or chopped pickle, mayonnaise to moisten, salt and pepper to taste. Add dry or prepared mustard instead of onion or pickle, if preferred.

8. EGG-BEAN SPROUT FILLING. Combine and mix 3 cut-up hard-cooked eggs, $\frac{1}{4}$ cup well-drained bean sprouts, mayonnaise to moisten, and salt and pepper to taste. Add ginger, if you like.

9. EGG-SESAME SEED FILLING. Combine and mix 3 cut-up hard-cooked eggs, $\frac{1}{4}$ cup ground and toasted sesame seeds, 2 tablespoons each of finely chopped carrot and celery, mayonnaise-yogurt combination to moisten, and salt and pepper to taste. VARIATION: In place of sesame seeds, try a combination of ground and toasted sesame seeds and toasted sunflower seeds.

Suggested Lunch Box Menu

Egg Salad Sandwich on Rye Bread
Mixed Green Salad   French Dressing
Orange   Oatmeal Cookies
Coffee, Tea, or Milk

For those who want more:
Lentil Soup and/or another sandwich.

What's Your Favorite?

These are just a few of the egg combination fillings to make lunch flavorful, interesting, and an adventure rather than a bore. Try, too, combination sandwiches. Instead of using a full portion of egg salad sandwich filling, use half the amount and top with a thin slice of ham, sardines, cheese, chicken, etc. Try your hand at other egg combinations. For a start, see what egg salad sandwich filling you can create using anchovies, cheese; different raw or cooked vegetables, seafood such as herring, salmon, tuna, shrimp, crab, or lobster, and meats such as tongue, chicken, and liver. Good eating!

___Toter's Own Favorite Egg Salad Sandwich Filling___

TASTE AND TEXTURE TIP. Overmixing sandwich fillings makes them like paste. They lack character because of the poor texture contrast, and the contrasts in flavors are lost, too. In a sense, they become highly processed. Why destroy the joy of eating that comes with differences in food textures and the mingling and blending of food flavors?

How to Pack the Egg Salad Sandwich Menu

If you like the idea of taking the sandwich ingredients separately and assembling a sandwich at the point of eating, pack this way:

EGG SALAD FILLING. Pack in prechilled wide-mouth vacuum bottle, plastic container, or other liquid-tight container. When using plastic or other type containers, pack salad in the container the night before. Refrigerate until ready to pack lunch.

BREAD. Bread may be packed with buttered sides together. Pack in wrap of your choice, or you may pack the butter or other spread in a small plastic container or small jar such as a baby-food jar.

ALTERNATE SANDWICH PACK. If, on the other

hand, you complete the sandwich at home, follow previous directions, and use the drugstore wrap as detailed on page 16, omitting freezer tape and using a nonfreezer wrap.

MIXED GREEN SALAD. Pack in plastic bowl or other container with tight cover.

SALAD DRESSING. Pack in small jar or plastic container with leakproof, liquid-tight cover.

ORANGE. Use nature's packaging or wrap of your choice.

OATMEAL COOKIES. Use the wrap of your choice.

COFFEE, TEA, OR MILK. Carry in a vacuum bottle, preheated or prechilled.

Pack salt, pepper, napkins, and whatever else you need to put together lunch where and when you eat. Include knife or spatula for spreading sandwich filling, and fork for salad.

TIP. Regular lunch toters keep a lunch kit in a locker, desk drawer, lunchroom, or other place where lunch is eaten. The kit holds fork, spoon, knife, salt and other seasonings, napkins, paper towels, can opener, beverage makings such as tea bags, instant coffee, etc. Some keep a plate, salad bowl, and cup, if foods are packed in containers or bags that cannot act as serving containers.

2. THE MEAT SANDWICH

The meat sandwich is the second most popular of the Super Six. Good taste. Good nutrition. Good for the lunch box packer who is in a hurry.

The thoughtful meat sandwich maker takes a long look at the choice of meat for the sandwich. Luncheon cold meat cuts such as bologna are easy, but here's something to think about. One ounce of cooked beef roast (heel of round cut) has 30 calories less than 1 ounce of bologna, $2\frac{2}{3}$ times *more protein,* and $2\frac{1}{2}$ times more iron! As you can see, you get less nutrition and you often pay more than when meats are cooked at home. It's so easy to plan meats for lunch box sandwiches from one's own home cooking. Plan ahead for three or four extra slices when roasting or simmering dinner veal, pork, beef, tongue, corned beef, lamb, ham, venison or other game. The taste is great, the eating pleasure is high, and the cost is much kinder to the purse.

Here's a taste factor that some people overlook. Thinly sliced meats make better sandwiches than when just one thick slice of meat is used. That's why many people enjoy delicatessen sandwiches—the meat is sliced so thin. Thinner slices release meat flavor to your taste buds more quickly than one thick slice.

About the Bread

Pair these delicious meats with bread partners such as pumpernickel, cracked wheat, cheese bread, whole wheat, oatmeal bread, and crusty breads such as Italian and French, and with flavorful insulator spreads such as suggested on pages 104-105. The lunch box will find new life —a variety of sandwiches stretching to infinity—an eating celebration every day!

Expert lunch box packers know that bread that has been chilled in the refrigerator for some hours cuts into the thinnest possible slices a lot more easily than bread stored at room temperature. Be sure to wrap bread well before storing it in the refrigerator to prevent it from drying out.

A serrated bread knife is best for cutting bread, but if you don't have one, use a knife with a long blade rather than a short kitchen knife. Short knives tend to hack the bread and compress the texture in a doughy, unattractive way.

Many Meat Choices

Roasts, pot roasts, boiled meats, meat loaves, and broiled meats all make delicious sliced meat sandwiches, and don't forget meatballs. Why not plan leftovers from sauerbraten, broiled steak, pot roasts of all kinds, stuffed flank steaks, Swiss steak, corned beef, "boiled" beef, beef brisket, pork roasts, pork tenderloin, hams, roast veal, veal pot roast, veal parmigiana, veal loaf, lamb roasts, lamb loaf, liver loaf, "boiled" fresh or smoked tongue, venison roast, venison pot roast, venison loaf, and other game. Go all the way with the bread, making sandwiches from open-faced to triple-deckers in addition to the conventional two slice kind.

Thinly sliced meats are also good combined with other fillings. Example: sliced pork, egg salad sandwich filling, watercress, and a curry spread on pumperknickel bread. That's good going for the lunch box! When people free themselves from humdrum lunch box packing, eating gets exciting and fun.

It's a good idea, too, to borrow some dinner combinations and put them between bread for interesting sandwiches. Here's an example from Boston Town. Use brown bread covered with a spread made by combining and mashing until well blended, drained baked beans, chili sauce, minced onion, and mustard. Add a thin slice of ham. When this Boston special is carried with a carrot and raisin salad, fresh or baked apple for dessert, and a beverage, there's great eating pleasure at a reasonable cost.

Sliced Meat Sandwich Suggestions

> Sliced meat, curried spread, whole wheat bread
> Sliced meat, black pepper spread, white bread
> Sliced meat, oregano spread, French or Italian bread
> Sliced meat, powdered rosemary spread, pumpernickel bread
> Sliced meat, savory spread, rye bread
> Sliced meat, chive spread, cheese bread
> Sliced meat, mustard spread, hard roll
> Sliced venison or other game, cranberry relish, whole wheat bread

Sliced Meat Sandwich Menu

Sliced Meat Sandwich
Tomato and Celery Salad with Dressing
Fresh Peaches or other Fruit in Season
Coffee, Tea, or Milk

For those who need more: Vegetable Soup,
an additional sandwich, and/or
Spice Cake

Meat Salad Sandwiches

When there isn't enough meat to make slices from a roast or pot roast, bits and pieces of meat can be chopped or ground to make delicious meat salad fillings. This saves a mint of money. Just compare with cost of little cans of meat spread. Check prices and you'll be amazed at how much you save making your own meat spreads. Besides, you get the flavors and trimmings that you like best in a sandwich when you make the filling yourself.

For this kind of sandwich, it's a good idea to invest in an inexpensive meat grinder if you don't already own one. If you do, just dust off the equipment and keep it in a convenient place. If buying a new grinder, you need not choose the expensive electric types. A hand grinder is

_Toter's Own Favorite Meat Sandwich _____

The Sandwich Case. When the Ladies Side-Saddle Hunters come riding gracefully into the arena at the Madison Square Garden Horse Show in New York, few people notice a little leather pouch that is part of the horse's accoutrement in this class. The little pouch is called a sandwich case. Though it is seldom used today, once it was part of every lady's prepara-tions for the hunt. The re-quirements were that it be filled with a simple sand-wich such as sliced chicken or turkey (no mayonnaise because of its perishable nature) and a flask of either sherry or tea. The crusts were cut off the sandwich to suit the dainty tastes of the day.

just as easy to use, much cheaper, and won't develop service problems.

Meat Salad Sandwich Fillings

     Ground or chopped cooked veal, grated onion, finely chopped green pepper, lemon juice, and mayonnaise

     Ground or chopped cooked tongue, prepared horseradish, finely chopped onion, and mayonnaise

     Ground or chopped cooked lamb, curry powder, and mayonnaise

     Ground or chopped cooked corned beef, finely chopped fresh cabbage and onion, mayonnaise

     Ground or chopped cooked pork, finely chopped onion and celery, barbecue sauce, mayonnaise

     Ground or chopped cooked beef, chopped mustard pickles, mayonnaise

     Ground or chopped cooked lamb with chopped fresh mint or mint jelly, mayonnaise

Ground or chopped cooked beef, tongue, ham,
pork, or veal with well-drained mashed baked
beans, piccalilli, finely chopped onion and
cabbage

Meat Salad Sandwich Menu

Meat Salad Sandwich
Escarole and Chicory Salad with Dressing
Pear or other Fresh Fruit in Season
Coffee, Tea, or Milk

For those who need more: Tomato Soup,
an additional sandwich, and/or Cupcake

3. TAKE THE HEROIC APPROACH

Heroes. Submarines. Grinders. Hoagies. Po'-boys.
They're all the same sandwich but the name varies according to where you live. They are made with a variety
of hard rolls or crunchy French or Italian bread. They are
hefty, robust sandwiches that satisfy the active person.
They can also be scaled down to size for the appetite of
the average toter. Varied breads and fillings as well as
crunchies, such as salad greens, tomatoes, pickled peppers,
coleslaw, carrot and celery salad, olive mixtures, cold
sauerkraut, etc., make each sandwich a special surprise.

To make a hero, or whatever you may call it, just split
a hard roll or crusty bread, coat with spread, add one or
more kinds of meat or poultry and cheese slices, salad
greens from escarole to watercress, and tomato slices.
Also include one of the following: pickled peppers, pickles,
relishes, mustard, or other garnish.

Heroes are quick-change sandwiches to suit your mood,
taste, and pocketbook. Try these for starters:

Hero Sandwiches

Bread, spread, cold sliced chicken, shredded
Cheddar cheese, cold sliced ham, egg salad,
shredded greens, sliced tomatoes

Bread, spread, cold slices of pork, provolone or
Swiss cheese slices, sliced tomatoes and shredded salad greens with zesty French dressing
(page 51)

Bread, spread, cold slices of veal and ham, or egg
salad, shredded mixed greens with blue cheese
dressing

Bread, spread, sliced beef or tongue, cheese
slices such as Muenster, Swiss, Cheddar, etc.,
turkey, mixed green salad with Thousand
Island Dressing (page 53) and sliced tomatoes
and onion rings

Bread, spread, cheese slices, liverwurst, slices of
cooked ham or fresh pork, shredded watercress and Boston lettuce mixed with herb
dressing

Hero Sandwich Menu

Hero Sandwich
Grapefruit or Orange
Coffee, Tea, or Milk

For those who need more: Tomato or
Vegetable Soup and/or Cookies

—Toter's Own Favorite Hero —————————————

How to Pack a Hero

When packing a bulky sandwich such as a hero or a club sandwich, insert toothpicks to hold the sandwich together. Then wrap drugstore-style or in plastic film wrap or aluminum foil. These wraps are desirable for bulky, irregular-shaped sandwiches because they cling to the uneven shape. Don't add crunchy materials such as tomatoes, greens, pickles, etc., and salad dressing. Pack these separately and add to sandwich at point of eating.

4. CHICKEN OR TURKEY SANDWICHES

Besides the popular sliced chicken or turkey sandwiches, there are the fabulous Club Sandwiches (below) made with three slices of bread. The bread is usually toasted, but this is not suited to toting. Instead, use untoasted, compact-style bread, rather than the puffy white kind, lightly coated with the spread of your choice. Almost any combination of chicken or turkey with other meats, such as tongue, ham, or beef, and cheese may be used to fill one-half of the Club Sandwich. Fill the other with crunchy greens, sliced tomatoes, and dressing, such as Russian.

Club Sandwich Combinations

Turkey or chicken slices and ham salad for one filling, and sliced tomatoes and shredded greens with Roquefort Cheese French Dressing (page 52) for the second filling.

Pastrami or corned beef and chicken slices for one filling, and sliced tomatoes and coleslaw for the second filling

Sliced turkey with Russian Dressing (page 53) for one filling and sliced hard-cooked egg on ham or sardine salad for the second filling, crunchies to suit your taste

Sliced Chicken Sandwich Menu

Sliced Chicken Sandwich
Finger Salad of Carrot and Celery
Sticks and Green Pepper Rings
Banana or other Fruit in Season
Coffee, Tea, or Milk

For those who need more: Potato Soup,
a second sandwich, and/or Apricot Squares

Chicken Salad Sandwiches

The traditional chicken salad sandwich made with
chopped or diced chicken, chopped celery, mayonnaise, and
seasonings to taste takes on new interest and flavor in the
following combinations:

Chicken salad and tongue
Diced or ground cooked chicken and diced cooked
ham or tongue, shredded cabbage, mayonnaise
to moisten, seasonings to taste
Diced or ground cooked chicken, chopped hard-
cooked egg, chopped olive or onion, mayonnaise to moisten, and seasonings to taste
Diced or ground cooked chicken, shredded sharp
Cheddar cheese or crumbled blue cheese,
chopped celery or grated carrot, mayonnaise
to moisten, and seasonings to taste
Diced or ground cooked chicken, chopped corned
beef, chopped celery and radishes, mayonnaise
to moisten, and seasonings to taste

Chicken Salad Sandwich Menu

Chicken Salad Sandwich
Spinach Salad with Dressing
Melon or other Fresh Fruit in Season
Coffee, Tea, or Milk

For those who need more: Bean Soup, an
additional sandwich and/or Fig Cookies

5. SEAFOOD SANDWICHES

The tuna sandwich leads all the seafood sandwiches in popularity. Having given it its due, consider also salmon, cooked white fish, sardines, herring, shrimp, crab, and other seafood. They all make marvelous sandwiches and help avoid monotony in lunch box packing. We hope you'll find some new ideas here that will inspire you to develop variations of your own.

For those who live in seaports or freshwater communities, where fish is less expensive, do take advantage of your opportunities.

Basic Tuna Salad Sandwich Filling

Makes 1 to 2 sandwiches

> ½ cup tuna (3-ounce can) broken into small
>   pieces with a fork
> ½ teaspoon lemon juice or vinegar
> 2 tablespoons mayonnaise
>   salt and pepper to taste

Measure the tuna into a small bowl or container. Add the lemon juice, mayonnaise, salt, and pepper. Mix until tuna is moistened. If necessary, add more mayonnaise. Recipe may be doubled.

VARIATIONS

1. In place of tuna, use salmon or any cooked white fish. Be sure to remove any skin or bone from fish.
2. Use sour cream or tartar sauce in place of mayonnaise.
3. Add to the basic recipe 1 teaspoon chopped capers.
4. Add to the basic recipe 3 tablespoons chopped celery. Add more mayonnaise, if necessary.
5. Add to the basic recipe mustard to suit your taste.

6. Add to the basic recipe 1 to 2 teaspoons chopped sweet or dill pickle.
7. Add to the basic recipe 2 tablespoons shredded cheese such as Cheddar or Swiss. Add more mayonnaise, if necessary.
8. Add 1 chopped hard-cooked egg. Add more mayonnaise, if necessary.
9. To the basic recipe add ½ teaspoon horse-radish, or to taste.
10. Use paprika in place of pepper to achieve an entirely different flavor.

Leftover Fried Fish Sandwich

Yes, you can use leftover fried fish in sandwiches. Cut into small pieces and follow the directions for Basic Tuna Filling.

Leftover fried fish also makes a great cold fishburger when teamed with sliced tomatoes, crunchy greens or coleslaw, tartar sauce, and rolls.

For those who have a kitchen at their place of work, pack the fish in a roll and wrap it in aluminum foil. Pack tartar sauce and crunchies in separate containers. Heat sandwich in foil at work. Add crunchies and tartar sauce. Presto, a hot fishburger.

The same thing can be done with leftover fried clams, oysters, shrimp, etc.

Sardine and Egg Sandwich Filling

Makes 3 to 4 sandwiches

> 1 cup mashed sardines
> 2 hard-cooked eggs, chopped
> 1 teaspoon lemon juice
> 2 tablespoons chopped pimiento-stuffed olives
> ¼ cup mayonnaise
> > or
> 2 tablespoons each mayonnaise and sour cream

Measure the sardines into a small bowl or container. Add eggs, lemon juice, olives, and mayonnaise. Stir and mix until mixture is moistened. Add more mayonnaise, if needed. Cover. Refrigerate until ready to pack.

VARIATIONS. In place of sardines, use salmon, tuna, or flaked cooked white fish.

Herring and Egg Sandwich Filling

Makes 3 to 4 sandwiches

> 1 cup chopped kippered herring
> 2 hard-cooked eggs, chopped
> 2 tablespoons finely chopped celery
> 1 tablespoon each of finely chopped green pepper, carrot, and onion
> ¼ cup mayonnaise
>   or
> 2 tablespoons each mayonnaise and sour cream

Measure the kippered herring into bowl or container. Add eggs, celery, green pepper, carrot, onion, and mayonnaise. Stir and mix until herring and egg are moistened. Add more mayonnaise, if needed. Cover. Store in refrigerator until ready to pack.

—Toter's Own Favorite Seafood Sandwich —————

Shrimp Salad Filling

Makes 3 to 4 sandwiches

> 1 cup chopped shrimp
> ½ cup chopped cucumber or celery
> 1 tablespoon chopped chives
> 1 tablespoon seafood cocktail sauce
> 2 tablespoons mayonnaise or tartar sauce

Measure shrimp into a bowl. Add cucumber, chives, cocktail sauce, and mayonnaise. Stir and mix until shrimp is moistened. Add more mayonnaise, if needed. Cover. Store in refrigerator until ready to pack.

Crab Meat Sandwich Filling

Makes 2 to 3 sandwiches

> 1 cup flaked crab meat
> 2 tablespoons chopped pimiento
> 2 tablespoons chopped celery
> 1 tablespoon minced parsley
> 2 tablespoons mayonnaise or tartar sauce

Measure the crab meat into a bowl. Add the pimiento, celery, parsley, and mayonnaise. Stir and mix until crab meat is moistened. Add more mayonnaise, if needed. Cover. Store in refrigerator until ready to pack.

Seafood Sandwich Menu

Fish Sandwich
Coleslaw
Fruit Cup
Coffee, Tea, or Milk

For those who need more: Pea Soup,
an additional sandwich and/or Cookies

6. CHEESE SANDWICHES

Another popular member of the Super Six is the cheese sandwich. It comes in dozens of different flavors, limited only by a person's proximity to a good cheese store or cheese department. Many lovers of good cheese sandwiches feel that individually wrapped cheese slices are almost tasteless, waxy, and without character. They prefer Cheddar, bought by the piece (also called store or rat cheese), or Colby, Swiss, longhorn, Muenster, provolone, and Jarlsberg, just for starters.

Look over the cheese area in your grocery store. When a cheese store is available, wander in and get a free education in cheeses of many lands and kinds. These cheeses make sandwiches with good taste, good nutrition, and eating pleasure. Don't hesitate to ask for a small taste before buying a cheese that appeals to you. There's no pleasanter half hour than one spent moseying around a fine cheese store or department.

Cheese sandwiches can be made with one or two different kinds of sliced cheese. Or try a cheese salad sandwich filling, alone, or in combination with meat, fish, or other foods.

For those who have a small kitchen at work, fix a cheese sandwich that can be grilled when you are ready to eat it. If there is no kitchen available, try this way-out idea.

Tina, a co-worker in the home testing kitchen of a major magazine, made a "grilled" cheese sandwich this way. First, she placed cheese between two slices of bread, buttered the outside of the bread, wrapped the sandwich in aluminum foil, and put it in the refrigerator. Later in the day when she was ironing in the laundry laboratory of the test kitchen, she took the sandwich from the refrigerator and gently applied the iron to each side of the sandwich in its wrapping until it was toasted. We had never seen a performance like this in all our years of working in a test kitchen. Tina served us a delicious grilled cheese sandwich. The secret was that she used a good sharp Cheddar of excellent quality.

Maybe you have an old iron that could still serve for this duty. Other workers have told us that although they do not have a kitchen in the office, their firms allow them to have a hot plate and a cheese-sandwich-maker grill.

This equipment was popular years ago. If you still have it, you might consider using it at work.

Don't overlook the "no-sandwich cheese sandwich." Take one or two kinds of cheese, pack the bread separately, and eat as you would cheese and crackers. Along with a finger salad, your favorite fruit, and the beverage of your choice, this makes a good lunch that is very quick to pack.

New Ideas for Cheese Sandwiches

Almost any kind of cheese lends itself to sandwich making, even those that are usually recommended for hors d'oeuvres, appetizers, or for cooking.

Those who like frying peppers and the blandness of Mozzarella cheese will enjoy this combination: Spread crusty bread with a black pepper butter spread, add salted cold fried peppers, shredded mozzarella cheese, and top with sharp-tasting crunchy greens, such as watercress or dandelion greens.

If this suits your fancy, you're pretty sure to like the combination of Swiss or provolone cheese with a leftover serving of eggplant parmigiana. Packed with a mixed green salad, an orange, and (go ahead, be good to yourself!) espresso coffee, this will transport you to Europe on your lunch hour.

For those who like Gruyère cheese, combine chunks of it with small amounts of a favorite potato salad and a few marinated shrimp. Make the bread rye or pumpernickel. Packed with a tomato salad and dressing, melon when in season, and something to drink, this makes a delightful tote lunch.

Something different, but simpler than these suggestions, is a ham butter spread for the bread, with slices of Swiss cheese, and crunchy greens of your choice. In place of the Swiss cheese, you may prefer Muenster, provolone, or sliced Cheddar. For more flavor, add mustard.

For those who like the salad-type sandwich filling, cut up or chop your favorite cheese, and add one of the fol-

Sandwich Geometry. For a change, it's fun to cut sandwiches into triangles, rectangles and other geometrics. Trim the crust and cut as illustrated. These are appropriate as finger sandwiches to go with salads. Children, in particular, like the novelty of finding their luncheon sandwiches cut into different shapes.

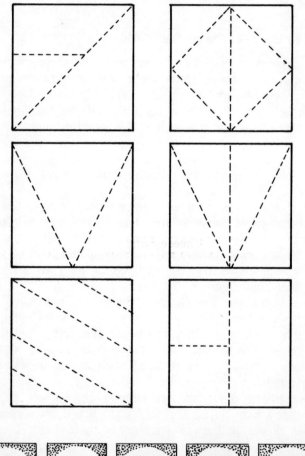

—Toter's Own Favorite Cheese Sandwich —————

lowing: chopped ham, chopped chicken, chopped egg, chopped shrimp, tuna, chopped olives or chopped pickle, and chopped celery. Add mayonnaise to moisten and seasonings to taste.

Cheese Sandwich Menu

Cheese Sandwich
Spinach and Boston Lettuce Salad
with Dressing
Tangerine or other Fresh Fruit in Season
Beverage of your choice

For those who need more: Vegetable Soup,
an additional sandwich and/or Pound Cake

PEANUT BUTTER PAIRS

The peanut butter sandwich is the youngsters' favorite. It's an American original. Peanut butter combinations range from A to Z—from peanut butter with apple butter to peanut butter on zucchini bread.

Those who eat peanut butter "straight" between two slices of bread draw back from real peanut butter buffs with their way-out combinations such as peanut butter and red caviar.

—Toter's Own Favorite Peanut Butter Sandwich————

Pick from these peanut butter pairs those that please you. Suggest the rest to the "P. B." buffs you may know who believe that any sandwich is good so long as it's combined with peanut butter.

PEANUT BUTTER-PICKLE RELISH. Spread each slice of bread with a thin coating of peanut butter. Top one slice with 1 or 2 tablespoons drained pickle relish.

PEANUT BUTTER-SLICED HARD-COOKED EGG. Spread each slice of bread with a very thin coating of peanut butter, top one slice with sliced hard-cooked egg and crisp salad greens; top with other slice of bread.

PEANUT BUTTER-EGG SALAD. Spread each slice of bread with thin coating of peanut butter. Fill with your favorite egg salad filling.

PEANUT BUTTER-RAISIN. Spread each slice of bread with a coating of peanut butter; sprinkle 1 or 2 teaspoons raisins on the peanut butter side of one slice; top with the other slice. Press slices together gently to prevent raisins from falling out.

PEANUT BUTTER-BANANA. Spread each slice of bread with peanut butter. On one slice of bread, add sliced banana to cover peanut butter. Cover with second slice. Press bread slices together gently to prevent banana from falling out.

PEANUT BUTTER-CARROT. Combine and mix well in

a bowl equal amounts of peanut butter and grated carrot. Use as filling.

PEANUT BUTTER-HAM. Spread one slice of bread with peanut butter and the other with a thin coating of butter. Spread buttered bread with ham salad filling. Top with other slice of bread.

PEANUT BUTTER-PINEAPPLE. Combine and mix well, ½ cup peanut butter with ¼ cup well-drained crushed pineapple. Use as filling.

Peanut Butter Triplets

PEANUT BUTTER-CARROT-RAISIN FILLING. Measure into a small bowl ¾ cup peanut butter and 2 tablespoons butter or margarine. Mix until smooth. Fold in ½ cup seedless raisins and ½ cup grated raw carrot. Refrigerate until ready to use.

PEANUT BUTTER-CHEDDAR CHEESE FILLING. Measure into a bowl ¾ cup peanut butter and ¼ cup apple butter. Mix until smooth. Stir in ½ cup grated Cheddar cheese and ½ teaspoon lemon juice. Refrigerate until ready to use.

2 salad_____
totes

For those who don't like sandwiches or want a change from sandwiches, salads make the perfect lunch box tote.

Main dish salads are so easy to make. A little leftover meat, fish, egg, fruit, or cheese combined with cooked or raw vegetables plus a peppy dressing—and there's your salad!

Main dish salads are often the most expensive item on restaurant luncheon menus. Made at home, they're yours for pennies. Following our tips, your main dish salad will be fresh and delightful at work when you're ready to eat it. Packing directions are included with the recipes.

On page 55 is a Salad Scanner with dozens of different foods for making delicious salads. Consult it to conjure up salads for your pleasure. Salads are among the most healthful of dishes.

Here are some very special salad recipes—the top favorites in our collection—but remember that you can improvise salads to your heart's content. The more original they are in their combination of ingredients, the more delight they will give you. Often, you don't need recipes. So fling culinary inhibitions to the winds, and fill your lunch box with salads that are a celebration of pleasant food.

40

Chicken, Mushroom, Deviled Egg Tote Salad

Makes 6 servings

        3 tablespoons mayonnaise
        1 tablespoon finely chopped onion
       ½ teaspoon crumbled tarragon leaves
        1 teaspoon lemon juice
        2 cups diced, cold cooked chicken
       ½ cup sliced cooked mushrooms, canned or
            fresh (well drained)
       ½ cup chopped celery
       ¼ cup shredded carrots
          salt and pepper to taste
        3 deviled eggs
 5 to 6 cups mixed crisp greens

Measure into a bowl mayonnaise, onion, tarragon leaves, and lemon juice. Mix until well blended. Add chicken, mushrooms, celery, carrots, salt, and pepper. Toss and gently mix until chicken and vegetables are moistened. If necessary, add a little more mayonnaise. Chill in refrigerator until ready to use. Pack a serving of chicken salad mixture in prechilled wide-mouth vacuum bottle. Top with ½ deviled egg and cover. Pack salad greens in plastic bag or container. If desired, pack salad dressing in small liquid-tight container.

VARIATIONS

1. In place of chicken, use turkey, ham, tuna, flaked salmon, shrimp, crab meat, lobster meat, or cooked flaked white fish.
2. In place of celery, use sliced radishes or chopped green pepper.
3. In place of mayonnaise, use tartar sauce.
4. Add mustard or chutney to mayonnaise mixture to suit taste.
5. Add ¼ cup chopped marinated artichoke hearts to mayonnaise mixture.

Ham-Vegetable-Cottage Cheese Salad

Makes 4 servings

> ¾ cup creamed cottage cheese
> 2 to 3 tablespoons mayonnaise
> ½ teaspoon salt
> ¾ cup diced cooked ham
> 1 cup cooked mixed vegetables
> ½ cup diced celery
> ¼ cup sliced green stuffed olives
> salad greens, if desired

Measure into a bowl the cottage cheese, mayonnaise, and salt. Mix until well blended. Add ham, mixed vegetables, celery, and stuffed olive slices. Gently toss together. Serve over salad greens, if desired.

Beef or Pork-Cooked Vegetable Tote Salad

Makes 6 to 8 servings

> 2 cups diced cooked beef or pork
> ¾ cup diced cooked carrots
> ¾ cup diced cooked potatoes
> ½ cup cut-up cooked green beans
> ¼ cup thinly sliced celery
> ½ cup French dressing
> 3 to 4 sweet pickles, chopped
> 2 hard-cooked eggs, chopped
> ⅔ cup mayonnaise
> or
> ⅓ cup each of mayonnaise and sour cream
> salt and pepper to taste

Combine the beef or pork, carrots, potatoes, green beans, celery, and French dressing in a bowl and mix well. Refrigerate for 1 hour. Add the pickles, eggs, mayonnaise, salt, and pepper. Mix well. Chill. Pack in prechilled wide-mouth vacuum bottle or other airtight container.

QUICKIE VEGETABLE MAIN DISH SALAD

For those really pressed for time, use cooked frozen mixed vegetables or canned mixed vegetables as a salad base. Just add any one of the following: chopped cooked chicken, cheese chunks, cooked beef cubes, chopped hard-cooked egg, salmon or other flaked fish. Add mayonnaise to moisten and salt and pepper to taste. Mix and refrigerate. Pack in a prechilled wide-mouth vacuum bottle.

VARIATIONS

1. Use blue cheese dressing or your favorite herb dressing.
2. Carry along a few croutons to add to the salad. Extra work but good eating.

POTATO SALAD—SIDE DISH AND MAIN DISH

Potato salad is an all-American favorite. When well made, it is a great addition to the lunch box. Good potato salad has a light, creamy dressing and each piece of potato is separate and distinct, never mushy. It's a snap to convert potato salad from side dish to main dish by merely adding a protein food such as meat, fish, or poultry. When ready to pack potato salad for the lunch box, measure out the amount to suit your appetite and add one of the following to make it a delicious main dish: 1/3 cup chopped shrimp, flaked tuna, sardines, minced ham, tongue, corned beef, pastrami, or any cooked meat, fish, or poultry that suits your taste. Mix into the potato salad, and if necessary, add a small amount of mayonnaise or mixture of mayonnaise and sour cream.

Pack this salad in a prechilled wide-mouth vacuum bottle, top with sliced pepper rings, radish roses, and carrot circles. Carry mixed greens separately. Arrange the salad on a plate at place of work and it will look as attractive as it tastes.

Old-Fashioned Potato Salad

Makes 6 to 8 servings

                ½ cup mayonnaise
                ½ cup sour cream
                1 tablespoon lemon juice or vinegar
                2 teaspoons prepared mustard
             1¼ teaspoons salt
                4 hard-cooked egg yolks, mashed
                4 hard-cooked egg whites, chopped
                4 cups of cut-up freshly cooked potatoes,
                      cooled to room temperature
                1 cup sliced celery
             ¼ cup chopped green pepper
             ¼ cup sliced green onions
             ¼ cup shredded carrots
             ¼ cup sliced radishes
                2 tablespoons chopped parsley

Measure the mayonnaise, sour cream, lemon juice, mustard, and salt into a large bowl. Add the mashed egg yolk and mix until well blended. Add the egg whites and potatoes. Mix gently to moisten potatoes. Add the remaining ingredients. Mix just enough to distribute vegetables through the salad. If necessary, stir in small amounts of mayonnaise and sour cream. Cover, and refrigerate until ready to use.

EXTRA TIPS

1. Use 1 cup mayonnaise in place of ½ cup mayonnaise and ½ cup sour cream.
2. Potato salad is best when made from potatoes cooked in their skins and peeled and cut while warm. Cool to room temperature. For best taste, do not use cold leftover potatoes in potato salad.
3. To avoid mushy texture in potato salad, use small waxy red potatoes, if available. They hold their shape and do not crumble when cut up.

4. When you are feeling adventurous, vary the taste of the potato salad by adding ½ teaspoon dill seed or ¼ teaspoon each of savory and oregano. If you like the taste of garlic, add ⅛ teaspoon garlic powder.

MACARONI SALAD—SIDE DISH OR MAIN DISH

Macaroni salad is another all-star American favorite. A sturdy accompaniment to lunch box sandwiches and soups, it's easy to convert to delicious and inexpensive main dishes by adding a protein food.

Measure out the amount of Macaroni Salad (recipe follows) to suit your needs, and add one of the following:

1. Small cooked meatballs; for real taste, make the meatballs very spicy, or if you really like hot food, try adding a little crushed red pepper; if you like Greek meatballs, add chopped mint to the meatball mixture.
2. Add ⅓ cup cooked chopped ham, flaked salmon or other cooked fish, tuna, shrimp, pastrami, mortadella, as well as leftover meats to suit your taste; for variety, marinate the cooked meat or mix it with a small amount of barbecue sauce before adding to the Macaroni Salad.
3. Don't overlook the use of cheese in making a main dish Macaroni Salad. One could make a different Cheese Macaroni Salad for every day in the year. Choose the cheese you like, shred it, and mix with the Macaroni Salad. When there are bits and pieces of cheeses, add different kinds to the same Macaroni Salad and enjoy the blend of flavors.

Pack Macaroni Salad in a prechilled wide-mouth vacuum bottle.

Macaroni Salad

Makes 4 servings

> ½ pound elbow macaroni
> ¼ cup finely chopped onion
> ¼ cup finely chopped pepper
> ¼ cup finely chopped carrot
> ¼ cup finely chopped celery
> ⅓ cup mayonnaise
> salt and pepper to taste

Cook macaroni according to directions on package. Drain well and place in mixing bowl. Cool. Stir in onion, pepper, carrot, celery, mayonnaise, and salt and pepper to taste. Add additional mayonnaise, if needed. Refrigerate.

EXTRA TIPS

1. Use sour cream and mayonnaise mixture in place of mayonnaise.
2. Do not overcook macaroni. Cook and cool as quickly as possible so that macaroni does not get soft and mushy. It's helpful to add a tablespoon of oil or fat to macaroni during cooking to aid in preventing macaroni from sticking together as it cools.

TUNA SALAD

Everybody knows this is a favorite salad with Americans, and everyone has a favorite recipe. Here's ours.

—Toter's Own Favorite Tuna Salad _____

Main Dish Tuna Salad

Makes 3 servings

> 1 can (6½-7 ounces) tuna, drained, and broken into pieces with a fork
> 1 cup cooled, cooked rice
> ¼ cup chopped pimiento or green pepper or celery
> ½ cup cooked peas
> ⅓ cup mayonnaise
> salt and pepper to taste
> crisp mixed greens
> garnishes such as radishes, cucumber wheels, etc., if desired

Measure the tuna, rice, pimiento, peas, mayonnaise, salt, and pepper into a bowl. Mix until tuna and rice are moistened. Add more mayonnaise, if needed. Cover and refrigerate until ready to pack. Pack in chilled wide-mouth vacuum bottle. Wrap and carry greens and garnishes separately and put together at eating time.

VARIATIONS

1. Instead of mayonnaise, use a mixture of mayonnaise and sour cream or yogurt.
2. For a different taste, marinate the tuna in French or Italian dressing and use as suggested in salad.
3. Combine the mayonnaise with 2 tablespoons of flavorful cheese such as Parmesan or blue cheese and mix until well blended.

MAIN DISH FRUIT SALADS

Toting fruit salads takes care. Many fruits are soft and perishable, bruise easily, and some discolor when cut. There is more than one way to solve this problem. You can go to the extra work of packing the cut-up fruit separately, and mixing the salad at your place of work, or you can take the fruits in their peel and cut them up and put them together just before eating.

SAMPLE. Fruit salad made by taking half a banana, half an apple, and a whole orange. Dip cut surface of fruits in lemon or orange juice to prevent browning. Pack in an airtight wrap. Pack greens separately and take a small container of cottage cheese or other cheese to top the salad to provide the protein lacking in fruits. Dressing, if desired, can be carried separately in a small container with a liquid-tight lid. Cut up and assemble salad at your place of work.

Cutting the Gordian Knot by Not Cutting

We have seen young people tackle the fruit salad tote in a simpler way. They just carry their fruit whole, bring a substantial chunk of their favorite cheese, and a sturdy dark bread, and eat their fruit, cheese, and bread in turn without having to do any cutting up or assembling on a plate. This makes a healthful and delicious lunch that lets you get out of the house fast in the morning.

The Melon Shortcut

When cantaloupes or honeydew melons are in season, make a very quick fruit salad by just cutting a melon in half, touching the cut surface with citrus juice, and packing in moisture-proof wrap. Take cottage cheese in a container and place in hollow of melon when ready to eat —a compact, delicious fruit salad that is a real quickie. The cottage cheese may be mixed with chopped raw or cooked vegetables, if desired, or with fruits. Nut bread is a good go-along with such salads. If you want to take the time, instead of cottage cheese, take a container of chicken or tuna salad and fill the hollow of the melon with that mixture at time of eating. Elegant, and very expensive, if you ordered it in a restaurant.

Mix-Aheads Are Juicier

Some people prefer the moister texture of a cottage cheese and fruit salad prepared the night before. Citrus fruit added ahead to cottage cheese flavors the cheese with its fruit and juice and makes the salad more moist. If you like, it will save you time in getting away in the morning to have the salad premixed.

Fruit Salad Tote Specials

Lunch box packers have found that frozen fruits do not carry as well as fresh, canned, or cooked fruits. They tend to lose texture for the most part.

Here are a few bright ideas for tote salads if you're willing to spend the time and effort to make them.

Rolyball Fruit Salad

Shape into 1-inch balls a mixture of shredded cheese, chopped cooked ham, and chopped nuts moistened with just a touch of mayonnaise. Take these in a separate container to serve over the top of a fruit salad made with fresh melon cubes, strawberries, and banana slices, or any fruit combination of your choice.

Avocado Picture Plate

Layer, in a liquid-tight container or prechilled wide-mouth vacuum bottle, citrus-treated avocado wedges, apple slices, orange sections, and a few blueberries or strawberries, packing the fruits in the order of their fragility with the berries on top. Dressing is carried in a separate container. Also pack finger sandwiches made with cheese or chicken salad fillings. When you are ready to eat, a feast meets the eye—avocado wedges on one side of the plate, red-accented apple slices next to them, overlapping bright orange slices, a cluster of berries for garnish, and the finger sandwiches to one side. All you need is a maitre d' hovering over you to complete the picture.

Summer Salad

A delightful fruit salad tote in the good old summertime is a combination of spiced fresh peach half, chunks of watermelon, and a pineapple slice served on mixed greens. Add a couple of prunes, if desired. To accompany this salad, take along finger sandwiches filled with chicken and watercress, or smoked salmon, or cheese and chopped nuts.

QUICK HOMEMADE SALAD DRESSINGS

Bottled dressings from the store are expensive, and they get used up so fast. You can make delicious salad dressings right at home and cut the cost by a third to a half compared to buying bottled commercial salad dressings or dried packet mixes. You may even find you have most of the ingredients needed right on your own shelves. Make up these dressings in advance for convenience, quality, great flavor, and great savings.

Salad dressings are a fascinating study, full of zest and variety. Think of salad dressing recipes merely as guides or starting points from which you may depart as you please. Personal preference determines choice as well as proportions of ingredients.

As an example, take a basic French dressing. It's a mixture of vinegar and oil with seasoning. Seems simple, but analyze it a bit further. For one thing, vinegar isn't just vinegar. It not only provides tartness in the dressing but also differences of flavor, depending upon the source of the vinegar. It may be made from wine, and flavor differs here, too, depending on the grapes from which the wine was made. The vinegar may be made from apples or from malt. It may be seasoned with garlic, or an herb such as tarragon, or spices such as clove, ginger, and nutmeg. Each makes a great difference in the flavor of the French dressing. Some people use lemon juice instead of vinegar for still another flavor.

There are many different choices in the oil to make French dressing, too—from olive oil to corn oil to safflower oil, each contributing a different nuance. Some people prefer to blend olive oil with a vegetable oil to make dressing.

The proportions of oil and vingear make a difference in the flavor and degree of tartness of the dressing. Three or 4 parts oil to 1 part vinegar produces only a slight tartness, while a dressing made with 3 or 4 parts vinegar to 1 part oil is very tart. When 1 part oil and 1 part vinegar are combined, the tartness is mild.

Here are zesty, flavorful dressings to send your lunch box salads to work in style.

French Dressing

Makes about 1 cup

$\frac{1}{4}$ cup cider vinegar
$\frac{1}{4}$ to $\frac{1}{2}$ teaspoon salt
$\frac{1}{8}$ teaspoon pepper
$\frac{3}{4}$ cup salad or olive oil

Measure the vinegar, salt, and pepper into a bottle or other container with a tight-fitting cover. Cover and shake until well blended. Add oil. Cover and shake until blended. If you like more tartness in dressing, cut the oil in the above ingredients to $\frac{1}{2}$ cup instead of $\frac{3}{4}$ cup. Refrigerate until ready to use.

VARIATIONS

1. Tomato French Dressing: Add 1 tablespoon tomato juice or tomato catsup.
2. Roquefort or Blue Cheese French Dressing: Add 2 to 4 tablespoons cheese, crumbled.
3. Anchovy French Dressing: Add 2 teaspoons anchovy paste and 1 tablespoon finely chopped onion.

4. Garlic French Dressing: Add a split clove of garlic. Remove garlic after one day.
5. Lemon French Dressing: In place of vinegar, use an equal amount of lemon juice.
6. Curry French Dressing: Add ¼ teaspoon curry powder.
7. Chutney French Dressing: Add ¼ to ⅓ cup chopped chutney.
8. Herb French Dressing: Add ¼ teaspoon marjoram and a sprinkle of thyme.
9. Wine French Dressing: In place of cider vinegar, use wine vinegar or wine.

Italian Salad Dressing

Makes about 1 cup

⅓ cup wine vinegar or lemon juice
½ teaspoon salt
sprinkle of pepper
1 clove garlic, split in half
½ teaspoon oregano
⅔ cup salad or olive oil

Measure the vinegar, salt, pepper, garlic, and oregano into a bottle or other container with a tight-fitting cover. Cover and shake until well blended. Add salad oil. Cover and shake until well blended. Remove garlic pieces after one day. Refrigerate until ready to use.

VARIATION. Parmesan Italian Dressing: Add 2 to 3 tablespoons grated Parmesan cheese.

Toter's Own Favorite Salad Dressing

Russian Dressing

Makes about 1¼ cups dressing

> 1 cup mayonnaise
> ¼ cup chili sauce
> 1 tablespoon finely chopped celery
> 1 tablespoon finely chopped pimiento
> 1 tablespoon finely chopped green pepper
> salt to taste

Measure the mayonnaise, chili sauce, celery, pimiento, and green pepper into a bowl or container with tight-fitting cover. Stir until well blended. Taste. If needed, add salt.

VARIATIONS

1. Pickle Relish Russian Dressing: Instead of chopped celery, pimiento, and green pepper, use 3 tablespoons pickle relish.
2. Horseradish Russian Dressing: Add 1 tablespoon horseradish.

Thousand Island Dressing

Makes about 1½ cups

> 1 cup mayonnaise
> 2 tablespoons chili sauce
> 2 tablespoons finely chopped green pepper
> 2 tablespoons grated carrot
> 1 tablespoon chopped parsley
> 1 teaspoon finely chopped onion

Measure the mayonnaise, chili sauce, pepper, carrot, parsley, and onion into a container with a tight-fitting cover. Stir until well blended. Cover and refrigerate until ready to use.

VARIATIONS

1. "Nippy" Thousand Island Dressing: Add ½ teaspoon chili powder.
2. Egg-Thick Thousand Island Dressing: Gently stir in 2 finely chopped hard-cooked eggs.

Coleslaw Dressing

Makes about ½ cup

　　½ cup mayonnaise
　　1 tablespoon lemon juice or vinegar
　　1 tablespoon pineapple juice
　　　salt and pepper to taste

Measure mayonnaise into a container with a tight-fitting cover. Add lemon juice and pineapple juice. Mix well and taste. If needed, add salt and/or pepper to taste.

NOTE. Try using ¼ cup mayonnaise and ¼ cup sour cream in place of mayonnaise.
For a tangy dressing, add mustard to taste.

Horseradish Dressing

Makes about ½ cup

　　2 tablespoons cider vinegar
　　6 tablespoons salad or olive oil
　　1 tablespoon fresh or prepared horseradish,
　　　more or less, depending on your taste

Measure the vinegar and oil into a container with a tight-fitting cover. Cover. Shake until well blended. Add horseradish and beat until well blended. Refrigerate until ready to use.

Pineapple Honey Salad Dressing

Makes about 1 cup

　　¼ cup well-drained crushed pineapple
　　2 tablespoons mayonnaise or sour cream or
　　　yogurt
　　½ cup honey
　　¼ cup lemon or lime juice

Measure the pineapple and mayonnaise into a container with a tight-fitting cover. Stir until well blended. Add honey and lemon or lime juice. Stir and mix until well blended. Refrigerate until ready to use.

Sour Cream or Yogurt Fruit Salad Dressing

Makes about 1¾ cups

> 1 cup sour cream or yogurt
> 1 teaspoon grated orange rind
> ½ cup pineapple juice
> ¼ cup finely chopped nuts such as pecans,
> walnuts, etc.

Measure the sour cream, orange rind, and pineapple juice into a container with a tight-fitting cover. Mix until well blended. Stir in nuts. Cover and refrigerate until ready to use. Fruit nectars such as apricot or peach may be used in place of pineapple juice.

The Handy Salad Scanner

Just to refresh your memory when you're looking for interesting, appetizing, and perhaps seasonal ingredients for salads, here's a selection:

Asparagus	Tender, sliced diagonally to use raw.
Beans, Green	Young, tender beans. May be used raw in salads; slice diagonally.
Bean Sprouts	Soybean or mung. Crunchy texture, tangy flavor used raw in salads.
Broccoli and Cauliflower	Break into small flowerettes; sharp, biting flavor yet crisp and tender used raw in salads; good marinated in tangy dressings.
Carrots	Use raw, coarsely grated, thinly sliced, cut in sticks, etc.
Celery	Shredded, sticks, cut diagonally.
Cucumber	Slices, spears, or cubes.
Green Peas	Shell; add to salad either raw or cooked.
Greens, Salad	See below.
Green Olives	Whole or cut-up.

Green Onions or Scallions	A young onion or scallion. Use tops and bulbs; tops add color, mild onion flavor, and nutrition to a salad; bulbs can be added whole or cut up.
Mushrooms	Wash just before they are to be used; store dry, unwashed mushrooms in a plastic bag or covered container to prevent withering; excess moisture and dampness cause mushrooms to mold or spoil. Do not slice mushrooms until just ready to use. This prevents discoloration. Dipping cut mushrooms in lemon juice or a dressing made with vinegar not only prevents browning but adds flavor.
Radishes	Keep best with tops removed; wash radishes, drain well, store in plastic bag. Tender radish leaves are good used in salad.
Sweet Peppers	Sticks. Chopped or shredded.
Tomatoes	A salad ingredient so well known, it requires no comment.
Zucchini	Use raw, cut into thin pieces to add to salad; may also be made into sticks and circles, and served the same way as cucumbers. White scallop squash may also be used in this way.

Other Salad Ingredients

Macaroni	Use cooked.
Rice	Use cooked.
Bulgar Wheat	Use cooked.
Water Chestnuts	Use raw, thinly sliced.
Bamboo Shoots	Cut into pieces or sliced; canned, or fresh from Chinese market.

Fresh Herbs	Chives, chervil, garden cress, parsley, basil, rosemary, tarragon, thyme; in addition, use savory, curry, cumin, chili, dill, caraway, celery seeds, mint, marjoram, cardamon.
Baked Leftover Pie Crust	Cut in odd-size pieces, sprinkle with garlic powder, sharp grated cheese, and seeds such as sesame and bake; these make excellent salad accompaniments.
Nuts	Pecans, walnuts, almonds, etc.
Cheeses	Old favorites include Roquefort and blue, grated Parmesan and Romano, to use in salad dressings; cubes and strips of many cheeses are added to chef's salad; cottage cheese is the old standby in fruit salad.
Croutons	Easy and inexpensive to make; delicious tossed with green salads and others. Croutons are simply bread cut into cubes, toasted in the oven or in a frying pan over low heat. While warm, add cubes to a paper bag holding garlic salt, paprika, and a sharp grated cheese such as Parmesan, and your favorite herb or combination of herbs. Shake. Voila! Croutons! Toss salad with the dressing, then just before serving salad, add crisp croutons and toss. Onion salt may be used in place of garlic salt.
Meats and Seafood	Flavorful pieces of meat and sea-food are perfect in a main dish salad or added to potato, rice, macaroni, or vegetable salads; a good way to use up bits and pieces of leftover meats.

Chick Peas, Kidney Beans, etc.	Cooked chick peas and other cooked dry beans may be marinated in dressing and added to salads; to save time, buy cooked canned beans, drain well.
Bonus Liquids	Instead of throwing out the liquid from pickles and olives, use it to marinate foods such as chick peas, cooked dry beans, raw vegetables for salad, sliced onion, etc. To add more flavor, use celery seeds, peppercorns, etc. When finished marinating, use the marinated food in a salad and make a flavorful salad dressing from the marinade —savings two ways.
Relishes, Pickles, Pimientos	Flavor perk-ups.
Special Breads	Toast in the oven or in a frying pan, flavorful cheese bread, crackling bread, etc. Add to salad in cubes. These breads have enough flavor without adding other flavorings, such as herbs, to the cubes.

Fruits—Fresh and Canned

Apples of all varieties	Limes
Apricots	Mangoes
Avocado	Nectarines
Bananas	Oranges
Berries	Papaya
Cantaloupe	Peaches
Casaba Melon	Pears
Cherries	Persian Melon
Cranshaw Melon	Persimmon
Figs	Pineapple
Grapefruit	Plums
Grapes	Pomegranate
Honeyball Melon	Tangelos
Honeydew Melon	Tangerines
Lemons	Watermelon

Tropical Fruits When Available

Breadfruit	Kumquat
Guava	Lychee
Kiwi	Plantain

Widen Acquaintance with Salad Greens

If you can possibly help it, don't be a "one green" salad maker. Some people never use any salad green but crisp head lettuce, such as iceberg, but there are so many other salad greens to enjoy. There's romaine lettuce with long, tapering leaves. There's escarole, a loose-leaved head, white at the base, dark green and ruffled at the tip. There's a slight nip to the taste that is very pleasant in a mixed salad. Chicory, or curly endive, as it is sometimes called, is frilly and fancy-looking. It's good by itself and it looks delightful in a tossed salad. Then there is Boston lettuce with flat leaves, loose rather than tightly bunched. Those living near farms may find field salad available, a tender, delicious green with small, oval leaves, or red-leaf lettuce, so colorful in salad.

Unfortunately, all these greens may not be available where you live but do look for them, learn to recognize them, and enjoy them for their contrasting tastes and textures when you can get them.

Many greens that are usually eaten only when cooked can make delicious salad ingredients if the tender or young leaves are used raw. These greens include mustard, kale, collards, turnip greens, and beet greens. Think of spinach, too, as a salad green. Use the leaves and tender stems raw. The dark green color and bitter-sweet taste are delightful in salads, eaten alone, or mixed with other greens.

Cabbage is best thought of as a salad green, considering its freshness, crispness, and pleasant range of flavors. There are four main kinds: the familiar green cabbage, red cabbage—which is really a handsome purple—that looks beautiful in salad, the savoy cabbage with crinkled leaves, and celery, or Chinese, cabbage, long and tapered with a crunchy, delicious texture. This cabbage is good with the stems cut into pieces like celery for salads. The other cabbages are best shredded or grated for salad use. Since the vitamin C in shredded cabbage is quite stable, coleslaw can be prepared ahead for lunch box use without a great loss of the vitamin.

How to Fix Salad Greens Ahead to Keep Fresh and Crisp

Fresh green salads taste so good and are so good for health, the best idea is to have the greens ready to use in the refrigerator at all times. Here's the way to fix salad greens so that they will keep fresh and crisp in most refrigerators for from five days to a week.

First, throw away any bruised parts that are wilted or have insect damage. Wash in cold water by moving the salad greens back and forth in the water. This will remove any dirt or dust or small insects that may be there. Take the salad greens out of the water and rinse in fresh water a second time. Take the salad greens out of the water and shake well. Allow them to stand in a strainer or your dish rack until the water has run out. Moisten a clean dish towel, wrap the salad greens in the dish towel, and place in a covered container or a plastic bag. Store in refrigerator.

Don't store greens unwrapped in the hydrator of your refrigerator. Air gets into the hydrator and takes the moisture out of the salad greens; they will wilt and spoil in a very short time. There is so much waste because of this practice. When you follow the directions given above, the salad greens will be crisp and crunchy, and will keep for a longer period of time.

Never cut or break up salad greens before storing them. When you do, the salad greens start to spoil, wilt, and become slimy. Cut or break greens only when about to use.

Some greens, such as escarole, have so much sand at the base of the leaves that they have to be washed when used, in addition to the first preparation for storage. Allow time for this extra step.

Fix-Ahead Finger Salads: How to Make and Keep Them

Finger salads are combinations of raw vegetables such as carrots or green peppers cut in sticks, circles, or spears for easy eating. They add a garden-fresh taste to tote lunches, and good nutrition, too. Most toters find they need finger salad ingredients prepared ahead in quantity and kept in the refrigerator for grab-and-run lunch box use in the morning. Here's how to prepare and keep finger salads fresh and ready in your refrigerator.

READY-TO-EAT CARROT STICKS. When buying carrots, choose those that are stiff and relatively clean; never soft and flexible. It's better to buy small carrots. Larger ones are tougher and may have woody centers.

Clean the carrots by covering them with cold water and scrubbing them, if needed. Peel or scrape, if desired. Remove tip and base.

Place a carrot on a firm surface and cut in half lengthwise. Now place cut side down. Cut the carrot lengthwise into the thinnest sticks possible.

To store: Moisten a white paper towel, wrap the carrot sticks in it, and place in a plastic bag, or in a plastic, or other type, tightly covered container. Store in the refrigerator. If the towel dries out, just add a few drops of water to it, rewrap the carrot sticks, and re-store. These sticks should keep for four to five days.

True, there is some vitamin loss in preparing and storing carrots this way, but it is better than doing without them altogether in lunch boxes because they are not ready for packing.

GREEN OR RED PEPPER STICKS, READY TO EAT. When buying green or red peppers, choose those that are firm and fleshy. Flabby peppers or those with very thin

walls or spots have already started to spoil and good vitamins have been lost.

Wash the pepper, cut in half, take out seeds and white
part. Pat the pepper dry thoroughly; peppers start to
spoil immediately in high humidity. Cut the pepper lengthwise into the thinnest possible sticks. Store same as for
carrots. Some may prefer to use half the pepper for
sticks; the other half for seasoning in cooking.

Many other vegetables are enjoyable raw in finger
salads. Try zucchini, cauliflower, broccoli, asparagus. Cut
in small pieces and store as above.

3 portable _____
soups

If you want to know how popular toted soup lunches are, just look at what's happening to soup carriers such as wide-mouth vacuum bottles. They now come in three sizes, 10 ounces, 1 pint, and 1 quart, or a choice of soup carriers for the inactive eater, the active, and the very active. Men who take the quart container of soup often use it both for lunch and for an afternoon soup break instead of drinking coffee. With some good, earthy, homemade soup inside, the world begins to look better.

One thing about soup—once it's made, it goes a long way. Some of our friends make a big pot of a favorite soup and take some each day to enjoy for itself, or to go with a sandwich or a salad.

If you've never made soup, you may be surprised at how easy it is. For good soup, you need quality ingredients, and the simple know-how of putting them together. The soup pot is a grateful receptacle for bits and pieces of leftovers such as the bone from a ham or a roast, a half-serving of mashed potatoes, a cupful of carrots and peas, and a spoonful or two of green beans. When these small amounts of leftovers are added to a pot of vegetable soup during the last five minutes of cooking, they add up to good flavor and to pennies, and even dollars, saved.

There is a soup to please everyone. Use basic ingredients such as meats of all kinds, poultry, fish, dried beans, peas, eggs, milk, cheese, pasta, rice, etc.; flavor with herbs and spices to your taste for a great variety of soups.

So many people use game such as venison nowadays.

Don't overlook using pieces of game in place of a ham bone or sausage to make robust soups. The carcass left from turkey or chicken makes excellent soup and so do chicken necks, gizzards, and hearts. Real soup experts never overlook any food's flavor possibilities. For fish chowders, for instance, they take home the fish head, tail, and other trimmings, often left behind at the store. They add savor to the soup and cold cash to the purse. Other good foods to save for making soups are the drippings from a roast, the trimmings from vegetables, and those bits of leftovers in the refrigerator so often left to stand and be thrown away. Stash them in the soup and tote delicious lunches for less money.

True, you can buy and carry canned soups, but there is a difference in flavor in soups made at home. Taste and compare. You may want to find the time to make your own. Soup does take time to make but a cozy pot of soup smells great when it's cooking, and you can do lots of other things around the house while the soup simmers.

When pressed for time, bring out the pressure cooker that may be gathering dust, and put it to work to make some soups in short order. In a hurry, canned broths or soups can be enriched both in flavor and nutrition by adding bits and pieces of leftover cooked meat, chicken, or fish, or frozen, canned, or leftover cooked vegetables, cooked macaroni or rice, egg-drop mixtures, grated cheese, etc.

You can truly eat for pennies yet enjoy a savory lunch when you make soups yourself. A hearty soup with slivers of meat teamed with a finger salad, crusty bread, and fresh fruit in season, makes a meal that is nourishing and satisfying. It's compact, and it's quick in the morning. The soup takes no work to pack, just heating it and pouring it into a pre-heated wide-mouth vacuum bottle.

Meaty Vegetable Soup

Makes 8 servings

        beef bones with meat on them; turkey or
            chicken carcass; or backs, necks, and giz-
            zards of chicken (wings when available)
    2 cups canned tomatoes, mashed
        enough water to cover bones
    4 stalks celery and leaves, chopped
    3 carrots, chopped
    2 onions, chopped
    1 cup chopped green beans
    ½ cup shredded cabbage
    ½ cup lima beans, frozen
    ½ cup peas, frozen
    ½ cup corn kernels, fresh or canned
    4 sprigs parsley
    2 potatoes, cubed
        salt and pepper

Place meaty beef bones, carcass, or chicken parts in a large kettle with a tight-fitting cover. Add tomatoes and enough water to cover the bones. Cover and bring to a boil. Reduce heat and simmer for about 1½ hours. Remove bones from kettle and allow to cool. Pick off meat and return to pot. Discard bones. Add celery, carrots, onions, green beans, cabbage, lima beans, peas, corn, parsley, and potatoes. Add water to cover vegetables. Cover. Bring to a boil. Reduce heat and simmer for about 35 minutes or until vegetables are tender. Add more water if needed. Taste. Add salt and pepper to taste. Pack hot soup in preheated wide-mouth vacuum bottle.

NOTE. The vegetables used may vary, depending on the season, what you have on hand, and your vegetable likes and dislikes.

Soup Menu

Meaty Vegetable Soup
Whole Wheat Bread
Apricots   Cookies
Coffee, Tea, or Milk

For those who need more: Add Salad and/or a Sandwich.

Quickie Vegetable Soup

Makes about 4 servings

½ cup broth, chicken or beef
1 tomato, quartered
1½ cups well-drained, cooked mixed vegetables,
      frozen (thawed) or canned
½ cup cooked celery
3 cups boiling broth, chicken or beef
1 cup cut-up cooked chicken, beef, etc.

Pour ½ cup broth into blender jar. Add tomato. Blend.
Add thawed frozen or canned vegetables and celery gradually and blend after each addition. Pour blended vegetables into hot boiling broth. Add cut-up chicken and cover.
Lower heat and simmer long enough to blend the flavors
of vegetables and broth. Pack hot soup in a preheated
wide-mouth vacuum bottle.

NOTE. A good way to use leftover cooked vegetables.

—Toter's Own Favorite Soup_____

Split Pea Soup

Makes about 8 servings

    1 pound (16 ounces) dried split peas
    meaty ham bone, ham, or ½ pound
        smoked sausage, enough to provide
        about 1 cup cut-up meat
    1 onion, chopped
    2 carrots, chopped or sliced
    4 ribs celery and leaves, chopped
    1 large potato, diced
4 to 6 peppercorns, if desired
    1 bay leaf, if desired
    3 quarts water
    salt and pepper to taste

Examine and pick over peas to remove small stones, soil particles, etc. Rinse.

Place the rinsed peas, ham bone, onion, carrots, celery, potato, peppercorns, bay leaf, and water in a large kettle or Dutch oven, with a tight-fitting cover. Cover. Bring to a fast, rolling boil and reduce heat. Simmer covered for about 3 hours. Add more water from time to time, if needed. Before soup is to be used, remove meaty bone or meat. Cut meat from bone into small pieces and stir into soup. Discard bone. Taste soup and add salt and pepper, if needed. Stir and heat for about 5 minutes longer.

TIPS. Instead of using peppercorns and bay leaf for flavor, use whole allspice or thyme, or a pod of red pepper. In addition, you may want to add the grated rind of 1 lemon.

TIME-WATCHER'S TRICK. For quicker Pea Soup, heat canned split-pea soup and boost nutrition and flavor by adding ½ cup cooked vegetables such as carrots, celery, and/or potatoes with ¼ to ⅓ cup cut-up ham, beef, sausage, etc.

Split Pea Soup Menu

Split Pea Soup
Cheese Bread
Apple   Cookies
Coffee, Tea, or Milk

For those who need more: Add Salad and/or a Sandwich

Quickie Cream of Pea Soup

Makes 4 servings

2 tablespoons butter or margarine
1 tablespoon finely chopped onion
1 tablespoon finely chopped celery
1½ tablespoons flour
¼ teaspoon salt
sprinkle of paprika
1 cup milk or cream
1 cup chicken broth or vegetable water
1½ cups cooked fresh, frozen, or canned
peas, blended or sieved
½ to 1 cup chopped cooked ham or other
cooked meat

Melt butter or margarine in a medium-size saucepan. Add and sauté onion and celery over low heat until onion becomes transparent but not browned. Blend in flour, salt, and paprika. Slowly stir in the milk and broth. Stir and cook to just the boiling point. Stir in the blended or sieved peas and chopped meat. Heat to boiling point. Pack in preheated wide-mouth vacuum bottle.

Manhattan Chowder

Makes 4 to 6 servings

2 tablespoons vegetable oil
1 potato, cut into small cubes
1 carrot, cut into thin slices
½ cup finely chopped onions
1 cup chopped celery
1½ cups tomatoes
2½ cups water, juice from canned or fresh clams, or fish stock
½ teaspoon paprika
thyme to taste
1 cup cooked flaked fish such as cod or haddock,
or
1 can (8 ounces) well-drained, minced clams
salt to taste

Heat oil in medium-size saucepan. Add potato, carrot, onions, and celery and sauté for about 5 minutes (do not brown). Add tomatoes, liquid, paprika, and thyme. Cover and bring to a rolling boil. Lower heat and simmer for about 20 minutes. Add cooked fish or minced clams and salt to taste. Heat, uncovered, only until fish or clams are hot. Do not boil. Pack in preheated wide-mouth vacuum bottle.

NOTE. For more flavor, ¼ cup chopped green pepper may be added with the vegetables.

Manhattan Chowder Menu

Manhattan Chowder
Hard Roll
Honeydew Melon   Cookies
Coffee, Tea, or Milk

For those who need more: Add Salad and/or a Sandwich

Bean Soup

Makes 6 servings

      1 cup (½ pound) dried navy, marrow,
           kidney, or lima beans
        meaty ham bone, piece of ham or smoked
           sausage, enough to make about 1 cup
           cut-up meat
      8 cups water
      1 bay leaf
  5 to 6 whole cloves
  5 to 6 peppercorns
      2 carrots, chopped or thinly sliced
      4 ribs celery with leaves, chopped
      1 medium onion, chopped
      1 large potato, cut into small cubes
        salt and pepper to taste

Examine and pick over beans to remove small stones, particles of soil, etc. Rinse. Soak in water overnight. Drain. Place beans in a large kettle or Dutch oven with a tight-fitting cover. Add ham bone, water, bay leaf, cloves, peppercorns, carrots, celery, onion, and potato. Cover. Bring to a rolling boil. Lower heat and simmer 2½ to 3 hours. Stir the soup from time to time and add more water, if needed. Remove bone or meat from soup. Cut meat from bone into small pieces. Discard bone and return meat to soup. Taste and add salt and pepper if needed. Cover and simmer for 10 minutes longer. Pack in preheated wide-mouth vacuum bottle.

NOTE. During the last half hour of cooking, you may add ½ cup chopped cabbage or sorrel as well as a clove of garlic (with a toothpick inserted to make removal easier). The bay leaf, cloves and peppercorns may be put into a small cheesecloth bag and tied, to be removed when bone is removed.

Bean Soup Menu

Bean Soup
Pumpernickel Bread
Orange   Cookies
Coffee, Tea, or Milk

For those who need more: add Salad and/or Sandwich

Lentil Soup

Makes about 8 servings

1 pound (16 ounces) dried lentils
  meaty ham bone, turkey or chicken carcass,
    ham or ½ pound sausage (enough to provide
    about 1 cup cut-up meat)
1 large onion, finely chopped
2 carrots, grated or shredded
1 cup chopped celery and leaves
3 quarts water
1 clove garlic
1 bay leaf
1 pod of red pepper, if desired
  salt and pepper to taste

Examine and pick over lentils to remove small stones, soil particles, etc. Rinse. Place the rinsed lentils, ham bone, onion, carrots, celery, and water in a large kettle or Dutch oven with a tight-fitting cover. Cover and bring to a full rolling boil. Lower heat and simmer for 2½ hours. Add more water, if needed. Add garlic, bay leaf, and pepper pod. Cover and simmer ½ hour longer. Remove bone or meat. Cut meat away from the bone. Cut rest into small pieces and return to soup. Cover. Simmer another 30 minutes. Taste and add salt and pepper to taste. Remove garlic. Pack in preheated wide-mouth vacuum bottle.

Lentil Soup Menu

Lentil Soup
Crusty Bread and Cheese Wedges
Fresh Peach   Cookies
Coffee, Tea, or Milk

For those who need more: Add Salad

4 breads _____
for
lunch box
excitement

Bread follows soup here because soup and bread make such a marvelous meal—filling, earthy, joyful.

Homemade bread adds a whole new dimension to sandwiches, and as an accompaniment to salads. Really good homemade bread is so satisfying, it makes a wonderful snack in place of sweets.

Many people don't think of bread as an exciting part of lunch. It's just a humdrum extra. But once people realize how much breads can vary, they often think it worthwhile to make bread at home.

There are two basic kinds of bread to make at home—yeast breads and quick breads. Quick breads are made without yeast, and take much less time. They are lightly sweetened, so they can make a delicious dessert as well as a pleasant accompaniment to salads, or as bread for sandwiches that have bland, delicate fillings.

Our yeast breads provide contrast to the regular white bread available in the store. The recipes are foolproof if followed carefully. The Cheese Bread (below), when used in a sandwich with a crunchy vegetable or fruit mixture, is the basis for a main dish meal. The amount of cheese used in this bread qualifies it as a complete protein

73

food. As you may know, most breads cannot fill this need in themselves.

None of the yeast breads are made with sugar yet they have delicious flavor and texture. As for the quick breads, the amount of sugar in each of the recipes is from a third to a half less than the sugar specified in standard recipes. In addition, the quick breads are made with a combination of whole wheat flour and white flour rather than white flour alone. When whole wheat flour replaces white flour, the bread is more nutritious and the fiber content is increased.

Yeast Baking Tips

All ingredients should be at room temperature unless otherwise indicated in the recipe.

Use standard measuring cups and spoons rather than cups and spoons used at mealtime.

When recipe calls for warm liquids, temperature should be 105°-115° F.

When recipe calls for very warm liquids, the temperature should be 120°-130° F.

Never use hot water to mix or dissolve yeast or yeast-flour mixture. Hot water kills the yeast and the bread will not rise.

When bread is rising, an even temperature of 80°-85° F. is best for all but refrigerator-type dough. Never place rising dough on direct heat such as a radiator, and do not place it in drafts. Yeast doughs rise best in a warm place free from drafts.

Rising time must be checked each time yeast bread is made because the temperature and humidity of the kitchen may be different and can slow down or speed up the time.

100 Percent Whole Wheat Bread

Makes 2 loaves

> 6½ to 7½ cups unsifted whole wheat flour
> 2 packages of undissolved active
>   dry yeast
> 1 tablespoon salt
> 2½ cups very warm (120°-130° F.)
>   water
> 2 large eggs, at room temperature
> ¼ cup vegetable oil

Measure into a large mixing bowl 2 cups of the whole wheat flour, the undissolved yeast, and salt. Mix until yeast is evenly distributed in flour.

Gradually add the very warm water (not hot) to the dry ingredients and beat by hand for about 5 minutes, or beat for 2 minutes at low speed of electric mixer, scraping down sides of bowl occasionally. Add eggs, oil, and 1 cup flour. Beat by hand for about 5 minutes, or beat for 2 minutes at high speed of electric mixer, scraping down sides of bowl occasionally. Stir in by hand, ½ cup at a time, enough additional flour to make a stiff dough. Turn the dough out on a lightly floured hard, flat surface and form into a ball.

Knead the dough for about 10 minutes, until smooth and elastic. Place dough in a greased bowl. Turn the dough over so that the surface on top is greased. Cover with a heavy towel. Let rise in a warm place, until dough is double in bulk, about 60 to 70 minutes.

Punch down dough and turn it out on a lightly floured hard flat surface. Divide the dough in half and shape it into two loaves. Place it in two greased 9-by-5-by-3-inch loaf pans and cover with towel. Let rise in warm place until doubled in bulk, about 40 to 60 minutes. Bake in preheated 375° F. oven for 5 minutes. Reduce oven temperature to 350° F. and bake for 35 to 45 minutes longer, or until done. Remove from pans and wrap in towels. Cool on wire rack.

NOTE. As you knead it, the 100 percent whole wheat dough feels different from bread made with white flour or white flour mixed with whole wheat flour.

Cheese Bread

Makes 2 loaves

> 6½ to 7½ cups unsifted enriched flour
> 1 tablespoon salt
> 2 packages undissolved active dry yeast
> 2⅔ cups very warm (120°-130° F.) water
> 3 cups (¾ pound) shredded sharp Cheddar cheese
> melted butter or margarine

Measure 2 cups of the flour, salt, and undissolved yeast into a large mixing bowl. Mix until yeast is evenly distributed in flour.

Gradually add the very warm (not hot) water to the dry ingredients and beat by hand for about 5 minutes, or beat 2 minutes at medium speed of electric mixer, scraping down bowl occasionally. Add cheese and 1 cup flour. Beat hard by hand for 5 minutes, or beat at high speed of electric mixer for 2 minutes, scraping down bowl occasionally. Stir in by hand just enough additional flour, ½ cup at a time, to make a stiff dough. Turn the dough out on a lightly floured hard, flat surface and form it into a ball.

Knead the dough for 10 minutes until smooth and elastic. Place dough in a greased warm bowl. Turn over so that top surface becomes greased. Cover with clean heavy dish towel. Let rise in a warm place until double in bulk, about 1 hour.

Punch down dough. Turn out on a lightly floured hard, flat surface and divide in half.

Shape the dough into two loaves and place in two greased 9-by-5-by-3-inch loaf pans. Cover with towel. Let rise in warm place until double in bulk, about 40 to 60 minutes. Bake on lowest rack position in preheated 375° F. oven for about 40 to 50 minutes, or until done. Remove from pans and cool on wire racks. Brush tops with melted butter or margarine.

NOTE. Because of the cheese, the bread is moist, compact, and dense in comparison to other yeast breads.

Oatmeal Bread

Makes 2 loaves

2 packages active dry yeast
½ cup warm (105° F.-115° F.) water, not hot
1 cup oatmeal (raw, not cooked)
1 tablespoon salt
1½ cups boiling water
2 tablespoons honey or molasses
½ cup vegetable oil
6 cups unbleached, enriched flour, approximately
3 tablespoons wheat germ
3 tablespoons unprocessed bran
2 eggs, beaten

Dissolve yeast in warm (not hot) water. Set aside.

Measure the dry oatmeal and salt into large mixing bowl.

Add boiling water and mix thoroughly. Stir in the honey or molasses and oil. Mix until well blended.

Stir in 2 cups of the flour, wheat germ, bran, and beaten eggs. Beat hard by hand until well blended, about 5 minutes. Add yeast mixture and beat hard again. Add and stir in just enough of the remaining flour, ½ cup at a time, to make a soft dough. Turn the dough out on a lightly floured hard, flat surface. Knead for about 10 minutes until smooth and elastic. Place in greased bowl. Turn over so that top surface of dough becomes greased. Cover with clean dish towel. Allow to rise until double in bulk, about 1 hour. Punch down. Divide in half and shape into two loaves. Place in greased 9-by-5-by-3-inch loaf pans. Cover. Let rise until double in bulk, about 40 to 60 minutes. Bake in preheated 350° F. oven for 35 to 45 minutes, or until done. Remove from pan and cool on wire rack. If desired, brush top of bread with butter or margarine.

French Bread

Makes 3 to 4 loaves

```
6 to 7  cups enriched flour
     1  tablespoon salt
     1  package undissolved active dry yeast
     2  cups very warm (120° F. to 130° F.)
          water
2 or 3  tablespoons corn meal
     1  cup ice water
```

Measure into a bowl 2 cups of the flour, salt, and undissolved yeast. Mix until yeast is evenly distributed throughout the flour. Add the very warm (not hot) water and beat by hand for about 5 minutes, or beat 2 minutes at medium speed of electric mixer, scraping down bowl occasionally.

Add 1 cup flour. Beat by hand for about 5 minutes, or beat for 2 minutes at high speed of electric mixer, scraping down bowl occasionally. Stir in, by hand, ½ cup at a time, just enough flour to make a stiff dough. Turn the dough out on a lightly floured hard, flat surface and form into a ball. Allow to rest for about 5 minutes. Knead the dough for about 10 minutes, until smooth and elastic. Place dough in a large greased bowl. Turn so that top surface of dough becomes greased. Cover with a heavy towel. Set in a warm place until dough triples in bulk, which should take 2½ to 3 hours, depending on room temperature. Punch down dough. Cover. Let rise a second time until double in bulk, about 50 to 60 minutes. Punch down again. Loosen dough from side of bowl with rubber spatula. Turn out on lightly floured hard, flat surface and knead for a few minutes. Cut into three or four equal pieces. Knead each piece a few minutes. Roll each piece back and forth with palms of hands, sliding hands gradually toward ends as dough lengthens. Shape each loaf 15 inches long or a length to fit baking sheets. Sprinkle greased baking sheets with corn meal. Place shaped bread on sheets. Using a razor blade or very sharp knife, make three or four long diagonal slashes in each loaf, about 3 inches apart. Let dough rise, uncovered, in a warm place until double in bulk, about 2 hours. About 5 minutes before placing bread in oven, heat oven to 400° F. Put a shallow pan on the bottom shelf and add boiling water to the pan. This provides steam, which helps create a crispy crust. Just before placing bread in oven, brush each loaf with ice-cold water. Bake bread for 20 minutes and brush with cold water again. Bake an additional 20 minutes or until bread is crisp, brown, and done. Remove from baking sheets and allow to cool thoroughly on wire rack.

—Toter's Own Favorite Bread ———————————————

Salt Sticks

Makes 24 sticks or 24 rolls

> 3 cups sifted, unbleached, enriched flour
> ¾ teaspoon salt
> 1 package undissolved active dry yeast
> ⅔ cup milk
> ⅓ cup butter, margarine, or oil
> 3 eggs, at room temperature
>   coarse salt

Measure 1 cup of the flour, ¾ teaspoon salt, and the active dry yeast into a large mixing bowl. Mix until yeast is evenly distributed in flour.

Measure the milk and butter, margarine or oil into a small saucepan. Heat until butter is melted and the mixture is very warm, 120° F. to 130° F. If hot, cool to very warm. Stir the very warm milk-butter mixture into dry ingredients and beat until well blended, about 5 minutes, or 2 minutes at low speed of electric mixer, scraping down bowl occasionally.

Separate *one* egg. Reserve white to brush on the sticks. Place egg yolk in a small bowl. Add the remaining 2 eggs and beat eggs and yolk until well blended. Add to milk-flour mixture and beat hard until well mixed, about 5 minutes by hand, or 2 minutes at low speed of electric beater. Add, all at once, the remaining 2 cups sifted flour. Stir in by hand until a ball is formed and pulls away from sides of bowl. Turn out on lightly floured hard, flat surface. Allow to rest for 5 minutes. Knead for 10 minutes, until smooth and elastic. Place in large greased bowl. Turn so that top surface becomes greased. Cover with heavy dish towel. Allow to rise in a warm place for 2 hours. Punch down. Chill in refrigerator for 3 hours or overnight in a tightly covered container. When ready to bake, remove from refrigerator and divide dough in half. Cut each half into twelve equal pieces. Shape each piece into a rope about 6 inches long. Place on greased baking sheets, about 2 inches apart. Allow to rise, uncovered, in a warm place for about 30 minutes, or until sticks have almost doubled in bulk. Brush sticks with a slightly beaten mixture of the reserved egg white and ½ tablespoon very cold water. Sprinkle with coarse salt. Bake in a preheated 400° F. oven for 15 to 20 minutes or until golden brown and done.

NOTE. For salt stick rolls, divide the chilled dough in half. Roll each half into a 9-inch circle. Cut each circle into twelve pie-shaped wedges. Roll up each piece beginning at the wide end. Arrange the rolls on greased baking sheet so the pointed end of the wedge rests on the sheet and the rolls are 2 inches apart. Allow to rise, uncovered, until double in bulk. Brush with egg white-water mixture. Sprinkle with coarse salt. Bake in a 400° F. preheated oven for 15 to 20 minutes, or until golden brown and done.

Date Nut Bread

Makes 1 loaf

> ¾ cup enriched, unbleached flour
> ¾ cup whole wheat flour
> ⅓ cup sugar
> ⅔ cup chopped, pitted dates
> ⅔ cup coarsely chopped nuts, such as pecans, walnuts, etc.
> 2 teaspoons baking powder
> ½ teaspoon salt
> 2 eggs
> 1 cup milk
> 2 tablespoons salad oil
> 1 teaspoon vanilla extract

Measure into a bowl, and mix thoroughly, the white and whole wheat flours, sugar, dates, nuts, baking powder, and salt. Set aside. In a second bowl, combine the eggs, milk, oil, and vanilla extract and mix until well blended. Add to dry ingredients and mix just until dry ingredients are moistened. Do not beat or overmix.

Pour into greased and floured 8½-by-4½-by-2½-inch loaf pan. Bake in preheated 350° F. oven for 50 to 60 minutes or until cake tester or wooden pick inserted in center comes out clean. When done, remove from oven and place on wire rack for 10 minutes. Remove bread from pan and place on wire rack to allow it to cool completely. Wrap. Allow to stand overnight. It tastes and slices better the second day.

Apricot Nut Bread

Makes 1 loaf

2 cups enriched flour
1 cup whole wheat flour
⅔ cup sugar
1 tablespoon baking powder
½ teaspoon salt
½ teaspoon cinnamon
¼ teaspoon nutmeg
   dash of cloves
1½ cups milk
1 egg
3 tablespoons vegetable oil
¾ cup cut-up dried apricots
   (use scissors for cutting)
½ cup chopped pecans or walnuts

Measure into a large mixing bowl, and mix thoroughly, white and whole wheat flours, sugar, baking powder, salt, cinnamon, nutmeg, and cloves. Set aside. Measure the milk, egg, and vegetable oil into another bowl. Beat until well blended. Add, all at once, to dry ingredients. Mix just until the dry ingredients are moistened. Do not beat or overmix. Stir in apricots and nuts. Spoon into greased and lightly floured 9-by-5-by-3-inch loaf pan. Bake in preheated 350° F. oven for about 50 minutes or until cake tester or wooden pick inserted in center comes out clean. Remove from oven and place on wire rack for 10 minutes. Remove bread from pan and cool completely on wire rack. Wrap.

Banana Bread

Makes 1 loaf

> 1 cup enriched flour
> ⅔ cup whole wheat flour
> ⅓ cup sugar
> 1½ teaspoons baking powder
> ½ teaspoon baking soda
> ¼ teaspoon salt
> ½ cup vegetable oil
> 1 cup very ripe mashed banana
> 2 eggs
> ¾ teaspoon grated lemon rind

Measure into a large bowl, and mix thoroughly, the white and whole wheat flours, sugar, baking powder, baking soda, and salt. Set aside.

Measure the oil, mashed banana, eggs, and lemon rind into another bowl. Mix with a fork until well blended. Stir and blend into dry ingredients with a fork just enough to moisten all the flour. Do not beat or overmix. Spread batter in a greased and floured 8½-by-4½-by-2½-inch loaf pan. Bake in a preheated 350° F. oven for 50 to 60 minutes, or until cake tester or wooden pick inserted in center comes out clean. Remove from oven and place pan on wire rack for 10 minutes. Remove bread from pan and place on wire rack. Allow to cool completely and wrap. Allow bread to stand overnight. It tastes better and slices better the second day.

5 the hot meal__
lunch
box

For those who want to eat their main meal from their lunch box in the middle of the day, it's possible to take a good, hearty hot dish and enjoy it like a dinner. But this is not quick food to prepare and pack. It will take time, just as getting dinner ready takes time.

People who hold two jobs, or who hold a job and go to evening classes, or hold a job and want to take advantage of an evening activity that requires going straight from work, usually favor this kind of lunch box meal. It allows for a quick pickup meal in the evening that costs much less than eating a main meal out.

Just as you have your shortcuts for preparing dinners, you can use the same time- and work-savers in making these hot tote meals. Almost any favorite meal can be packed by using the right size wide-mouth vacuum bottle. The food must be prepared in pieces that fit the neck of the bottle. For example, even chicken cacciatore finds its place in a lunch box meal when the pieces are cut smaller than normally. Instead of slicing pot roast, cut it in small chunks or cut slices into smaller pieces, and pack the meat in the gravy.

A whole meal can be carried in one vacuum bottle, using the "layered meal" technique. For example, a meal of pot roast and gravy with mashed potatoes and green beans can be packed in a preheated wide-mouth vacuum bottle with the beans at the bottom, the potatoes in the middle, and the gravy and beef on top. To keep the meal hot, pre-

84

heat the bottle by filling it with boiling water, cover, and allow to stand for five minutes. Empty the bottle and fill it with the hot food.

Hot main meals are also a blessing for people who work the night shift. Many people find it hard to get up and eat dinner before going to work. With a little flexibility and the right equipment, one can pack the kind of meal that suits his or her work hours. Some people even carry a hearty breakfast in the wide-mouth vacuum bottle, and this is their main meal of the working day. They take an individual-pack orange juice, frozen in the can or a plastic container, hot oatmeal in a preheated wide-mouth vacuum bottle, a cheese or egg sandwich, and something else to drink, such as tea or coffee. Remember, pack hot meals only just before leaving home.

Hot Breakfast Tote Meal

Tomato Juice
Hot Oatmeal   Brown Sugar
Cheese, Ham, or Egg Sandwich
Baked Apple
Coffee, Tea, or Milk

Vacuum Bottle Oatmeal

Makes 1 large serving

1¾ cups water
¼ to ½ teaspoon salt
½ cup old-fashioned rolled oats (oatmeal)

Measure the water and salt into a saucepan. Bring to a brisk, rolling boil. Stir the dry oatmeal into the boiling water. Cook for 5 minutes, stirring occasionally. Cover. Remove from heat and let stand for 2 minutes. Spoon hot oatmeal into a preheated wide-mouth vacuum bottle and cover. Pack sugar and milk separately, if you use them.

NOTE. Oatmeal should be on the thin side. It will thicken while it travels in the vacuum bottle. When using quick-cooking rolled oats, decrease the water to 1¼ cups. Cook just 1 minute, following the directions above.

Tips on Packing Breakfast Meal

1. Freeze small can of tomato juice, or freeze tomato juice in a leakproof, liquid-tight container. Pack into lunch box. It will thaw by eating time, and help keep food cold.
2. Pack oatmeal in preheated wide-mouth vacuum bottle. Pack sugar in wrap, small plastic bag, or small container.
3. Pack sandwich in wrap, sandwich bag, or plastic sandwich container.
4. Pack baked apple in prechilled snack thermo jar, wide-mouth vacuum bottle, or other container. For hot apple, pack in preheated wide-mouth vacuum bottle.
5. Pack coffee, tea, or milk in preheated or prechilled vacuum bottle, depending on your choice of beverage.

Chili con Carne

Makes 6 to 8 servings

1	tablespoon salad oil
2	pounds lean coarsely ground beef, or beef cut into very small cubes
1	cup chopped onion
½	cup finely chopped celery leaves
½	cup finely chopped green pepper
1	garlic clove, finely minced
1	can (2 pounds 3 ounces) canned tomatoes and liquid
4 to 6	tablespoons chili powder to taste
2	teaspoons salt
2	cans (1 pound to 1 pound 4 ounces each) kidney beans and liquid
	additional salt, if needed

Place the salad oil in a Dutch oven or large heavy pan with a tight-fitting cover over medium-high heat. When oil is hot, add the meat, chopped onion, celery leaves, green pepper, and garlic. Cook, stirring frequently, until onion is tender. Add tomatoes and liquid, chili powder, and salt. Bring to a boil. Cover. Lower heat and simmer for 45 minutes.

Stir in beans and liquid and bring to a boil. Cover. Lower heat and simmer 30 minutes longer, stirring occasionally to prevent sticking. Taste. Add more salt if needed. Cool and refrigerate until ready to use.

TO PACK CHILI. Spoon portion or portions of chili into a saucepan. Heat over medium-low heat until hot. Spoon into preheated wide-mouth vacuum bottle and cover.

May be served with cooked rice or macaroni, if desired.

Main Dish Fried Rice

Makes 4 to 6 servings

3	tablespoons oil or drippings
2	eggs
¼	cup finely diced onion
1½	cups finely chopped cooked shrimp, ham, or pork
	salt to taste
	dash of pepper
4	cups cooked rice
2 to 3	tablespoons soy sauce

Heat oil in a large skillet. Add eggs and fry. Turn and cook until yolk is firm. Remove from heat and cut fried eggs in the pan into shreds. Move shredded eggs to side of the skillet. Add onion, shrimp, ham, or pork, salt, and pepper to skillet. Return to heat. Cook over medium heat, stirring the onion and shrimp constantly, until onion is tender. Add rice. Gently mix rice, shrimp mixture, and egg. Sprinkle soy sauce over rice. Cook over medium heat, stirring until rice is hot.

To pack for tote lunch, spoon hot fried rice into a preheated wide-mouth vacuum bottle. Cover.

NOTE. To reheat fried rice, add about 1 to 2 tablespoons broth or water to each portion. This helps to keep the rice moist.

Lemon Chicken

Makes 4 to 6 servings

  1 whole (2½ to 3 pounds) broiler/fryer, cut into pieces to fit wide-mouth vacuum bottle
  4 slices bacon, cut into 2-inch pieces
  1 or two lemons, sliced
  4 carrots, quartered lengthwise, and cut into 2-inch lengths
  2 medium onions, sliced into circles
1½ cups chicken broth or water
  ½ teaspoon thyme or oregano
  ¼ teaspoon allspice
  ⅛ teaspoon mace
1½ teaspoons salt
  ½ teaspoon freshly ground pepper, more if desired
  2 tablespoons finely chopped parsley
  1 bay leaf

If necessary, wash or wipe the chicken pieces clean with a damp cloth. Set aside.

Distribute the bacon evenly over the bottom of a Dutch oven or other heavy pan with a tight-fitting cover. Place the lemon slices over the bacon. Use one lemon for a hint of lemon flavor or two for a stronger lemon taste.

Put in layers, over the lemon, first the carrots and then the onion slices.

Pour the broth or water over the onions. Sprinkle in the thyme, allspice, mace, salt, pepper, and parsley. Add the bay leaf.

Place the Dutch oven over high heat and bring to a boil. Add the chicken pieces and cover. Reduce heat and simmer about 60 to 70 minutes, or until chicken is tender. If the liquid evaporates, add additional broth or water. Taste about 10 minutes before done and add more salt or pepper, if needed.

PACKING TIP. Pack hot portion of chicken and vegetables in a preheated wide-mouth vacuum bottle.

NOTE. For those who choose not to eat bacon treated with nitrite, ask your butcher about nitrite-free bacon.

Hunter's Stew

Makes 4 to 6 servings

> 2 pounds sauerkraut
> ½ to ¾ cup cooked (canned, fresh, or dried) mushrooms, plus liquid from mushrooms
> 2 apples, peeled, cored, and sliced
> 1 can (28 ounces) tomatoes
> 10 peppercorns
> 1 bay leaf
> 2½ cups diced cooked beef, veal or pork, or smoked sausages ·
> ½ cup cubed salt pork or bacon cooked rice or steamed potatoes

Wash the sauerkraut in cold water. Press or squeeze out as much of the water as possible. Place the sauerkraut in a heavy pan or Dutch oven with a tight-fitting cover. Add the mushrooms, liquid, apples, tomatoes, peppercorns, and bay leaf. Cover. If necessary, add just enough water to cover the sauerkraut mixture. Bring to a boil. Lower heat and simmer for 1½ hours.

Add the diced meat and salt pork to the sauerkraut. Cover and bring to a boil. Lower heat and simmer 1 hour longer. Stew should be "soupy." If needed, add water. Hunter's Stew may be served with rice or steamed potatoes.

To pack for a tote lunch, spoon hot stew with or without rice or potatoes into a preheated wide-mouth vacuum bottle and cover.

NOTE. For those who do not use bacon treated with nitrite, ask your butcher about bacon available without nitrite.

HOT SANDWICH SUGGESTIONS

Sausage-Cheese-Pepper Hero

Cook up sausage, green pepper sticks, and sliced onions with a freshly sliced tomato. Season to taste. Pack in a preheated wide-mouth vacuum bottle. Spoon into a wedge of Italian or French bread or a hard roll at lunchtime.

Complete the meal with a finger salad of your choice, a piece of fruit, and something to drink. If your appetite calls for more food, add soup or dessert.

Meatball Sandwich

Spoon your favorite heated meatballs with tomato sauce or mushroom sauce into a preheated wide-mouth vacuum bottle. Cover. At lunch hour, spoon into a hard roll or other crusty bread. Presto—a hot hero!

Roast Beef French Dip Sandwich

Spoon hot thinly sliced beef and double-strength beef stock or bouillon into a preheated wide-mouth vacuum bottle. Cover. At lunchtime, fill crusty French or Italian bread with beef slices. Pour beef bouillon into a cup and dip sandwich in it. Happy eating.

6 the gourmet____ packs a lunch

Delightful gourmet go-alongs for the lunch box include scrumptious smooth soup such as cold Avocado Yogurt Soup (page 93) and the world-famous Gazpacho (page 94) from Andalusia, a superb Chef's Salad (page 95) with a very special dressing, and gourmet sandwiches exotic with anchovy, caviar, and other fancy fillings.

The gourmet lunch box packer has been known to entertain clients in her or his office with a feast for two. A complete antipasto lunch can be packed and shared, and it isn't that hard to get together since so many of the foods, such as meat, are ready-bought. Turn on the radio, tune in some classical music, and the dining is just as elegant as in an expense account restaurant. Only it's better because there's no reservation to make, no waiting at the bar for a table if you didn't make a reservation, and no cross-static of conversations because the tables are placed much too close.

When thoughts turn to gourmet lunch box fare, think of crab meat and avocado salad or Scotch Eggs (page 100) served with other foods on toothpicks for easy pickup. In Paley Park in New York City with its tall wall fountain of falling water, and by the Wharf in San Francisco, one often sees people who have packed a gourmet lunch

The Royal Lunch Box. When the Count of Blois and his party rode forth to hunt from Chateau de Chambord, his 440-room hunting lodge, the royal lunch box rattled after him in an elaborate coach down the splendid, tree-lined avenue in his 13,000-acre hunting park. One may imagine the luscious lunch the royal lunch box afforded, all done up in the inimitable French style—unctuous goose liver patés; glistening, amber-jelled gallantines; herb-scented meat patés, rich and velvety; creamy cheeses of the countryside; fabulous crusty breads; cold coq au vin; fowl sliced in thin shavings; and for salad, tomatoes au vinaigrette, lavishly strewn with fresh parsley. Don't forget the clink of the wine bottles as the royal coach rolled along. The Count and his friends dined well from the royal lunch box, once the hunting prize was won.

enjoying it outdoors. The same thing goes on at the Tuileries in Paris, where lunches of elegant meat or goose liver paté, crusty bread, and garden tomatoes appear in the park after the clock strikes noon. The Frenchman will often have a small, individual-size bottle of wine, smaller than a carbonated drink bottle, to go with his lunch. Why not pick up on these cues and enjoy gourmet lunches indoors or out, with elegant food prepared by your own hands.

Here are ideas to start you off. Consider your own favorites among the higher rank of edibles and see if you can adapt them to travel to work with you. We include packing ideas for our gourmet lunches.

Avocado Yogurt Soup

Makes 2 servings

> 1 cup mashed avocado pulp
> 1 cup yogurt or heavy cream
> 1 cup cold beef or chicken broth
> 3/4 teaspoon each of lemon juice and lime juice
> or
> 1½ teaspoons lemon or lime juice
> ½ teaspoon finely minced onion, or onion juice, if desired
> ¼ teaspoon chili powder

Force mashed avocado pulp through a fine sieve. Gradually stir yogurt and broth into the avocado. Add the lemon and lime juice, onion, and chili powder. Mix until well blended. If too thick, add a small amount of broth. Place in refrigerator and allow to chill thoroughly. When ready to pack for lunch, stir chilled soup until well blended and spoon into chilled wide-mouth vacuum bottle. Cover. Stir well just before you are ready to eat.

Blender Gazpacho

Makes about 5 cups

> 5 fully ripe tomatoes, peeled and cut into coarse pieces
> 1 small onion, peeled and cut into coarse pieces
> 1 garlic clove, mashed (optional)
> 4 leaves fresh basil
> 2 sprigs fresh parsley, coarsely chopped
> 1 cup chicken or light beef broth
> 3 tablespoons oil
> 2 teaspoons tarragon vinegar
> 1 tablespoon lemon juice
> 1/8 teaspoon paprika
> salt to taste
> finely chopped cucumber, mild onion, green and/or red sweet pepper
> seasoned croutons, if desired

Place about 1 cup cut-up tomatoes in blender. Cover and blend. Gradually add cut-up onion, garlic, basil, and parsley, covering and blending after each addition. Blend until mixture is smooth. Add remaining tomatoes, chicken broth, oil, vinegar, lemon juice, and paprika. Cover and blend until mixture is smooth. Should there be too much to blend at one time, blend only the remaining tomatoes and all the remaining ingredients except the chicken broth. Cover and blend as directed. Pour off 2 cups of blended mixture into a bowl. Add the broth to blender. Cover and blend until smooth. Add to blended mixture in bowl. Cover and refrigerate. Chill soup thoroughly. When ready to pack, spoon into prechilled wide-mouth vacuum bottle, 1/2 to 3/4 cup mixed fresh vegetables of finely chopped cucumber, mild onion, green and/or red sweet pepper. Pour chilled tomato mixture to fill vacuum bottle. Cover. If desired, pack seasoned croutons in wrap or a container, to be eaten with the gazpacho.

NOTES
1. You may decrease the number of tomatoes and increase the amount of broth to suit your taste.
2. For those who like a hot, spicy gazpacho, add ground red pepper or bottled hot sauce to taste.

Chef's Special Salad

Makes 2 servings

> 2 or more cups mixed greens such as Bibb and Boston lettuce, watercress, endive, tender raw spinach leaves, arugula, escarole, chicory, tender radish leaves, etc. Tear into bite-size pieces.
>
> enough cucumber, in one piece, to make 8 to 10 slices
>
> 2 whole radishes, to be cut into slices or made into radish roses
>
> 4 cherry tomatoes
>
> 2 slices onion, cut in circles and separated into rings
>
> 2 thin slices prosciutto or other ham, cut into thin slivers
>
> 2 thin slices Gruyère, Tilsiter, or other cheese, cut into thin slivers
>
> 2 thin slices smoked chicken, roasted chicken, or turkey, cut into thin slivers
>
> 2 small marinated artichoke hearts
>
> 1/4 cup cooked chick peas, seasoned with black or red pepper.
>
> small amounts of raw broccoli and cauliflowerettes, asparagus, etc., sliced at lunchtime
>
> carrot curls made at home

To Pack the Chef's Salad

1. Pack the cold crisp salad greens and cherry tomatoes in a mixing bowl with a tight-fitting cover. If you keep a salad bowl at work, pack greens and tomatoes in a plastic bag.

2. Pack the following in another container or plastic bag so that the heaviest ingredients are at the bottom:
   a. cucumber in one piece; to be sliced at lunch
   b. radishes, whole; cut at lunch
   c. onion rings wrapped in moisture-proof wrap
   d. chick peas packed in moisture-proof wrap
   e. broccoli, cauliflower, asparagus, etc., uncut. Cut at lunchtime. Top with the crisp carrot curls and remove wooden pick that holds carrot curls together at lunchtime.

3. Pack slivers of meat, chicken, and cheese in a prechilled snack thermo jar or other container.

4. Pack salad dressing in a tightly covered container. Chopped herbs for the dressing are packed in a separate small container.

Putting the Chef's Salad Together at Lunchtime

Place salad greens in mixing bowl. Slice and add the cucumbers, radishes, onion rings, chick peas, broccoli, cauliflower, asparagus, etc. Set aside.

Add mixed herbs to salad dressing. Cover and shake container until dressing is well blended. Add the amount desired to salad and toss salad gently. Divide into two portions and place on plates or in bowls. Add tomatoes and artichoke hearts to each salad. Top with chick peas, onion rings, prosciutto, Gruyère, and smoked chicken slivers. Each person may add additional salad dressing, if desired.

Special Chef's Salad Dressing

Makes about ½ cup

> ⅓ cup olive or salad oil
> salt and freshly ground pepper to taste
> 2 teaspoons wine vinegar
> 1 tablespoon lemon juice
> prepared strong Dijon mustard to taste
> 1 tablespoon finely minced fresh herbs such as
>   parsley, chervil, basil, chives, and tarragon,
>   or a sprinkle of dried herbs

Measure salad oil, salt, and pepper into a 1-cup refrigerator jar with cover. Stir until well mixed. Add vinegar, lemon juice, and mustard. Cover and shake until well mixed. Add mixed herbs just before you are ready to serve.

Chef's Seafood Salad

Makes 2 servings

> 2 cups mixed greens such as Bibb,
>   Boston, romaine, watercress, escarole,
>   etc. (Use 1 cup per serving)
> ¼ pound cooked and chilled crab meat
> ¼ pound cooked and chilled lobster meat
> 4 large cooked shrimp that have been
>   shelled, deveined, and chilled
> ¼ pound cooked white fish fillet such as
>   halibut, cod, flounder, sole, etc.,
>   that has been flaked and chilled
> 1 tomato, peeled and cut into wedges
>   black olives
>   green olives
> 1 hard-cooked egg, shelled and quartered
>   capers
> ½ to ⅔ cup seafood cocktail sauce or
>   mayonnaise dressing of your choice
> ½ lemon, cut into wedges

To make individual salads, arrange 1 cup of salad greens on each plate. Place half of the crab meat, lobster, shrimp, and white fish on each plate. Add the tomatoes, olives, and eggs to make an attractive arrangement. Sprinkle each salad with a few capers. Place lemon wedge on plates. Pass the dressing or cocktail sauce.

To Pack Chef's Seafood Salad

1. Place chilled olives in the bottom of a pre-chilled wide-mouth vacuum bottle. Starting with chilled crab meat, layer the chilled crab meat, chilled lobster, chilled shrimp, and chilled white fish. Place chilled whole hard-cooked egg on top—they are best when quartered at time of serving.
2. Place cleaned, crisped chilled salad greens in a plastic bag, or a container with cover.
3. Pack peeled tomato in wrap, -container, or plastic bag. It may be placed in bottom of the salad greens container. Cut when ready to fix salad.
4. Pack dressing in a liquid-tight plastic container.
5. Pack lemon in wrap.

LUNCH BOX ANTIPASTO MEAL

Antipasto means literally "before meal." For many Italians, it means the food served before the pasta. For the toter, it can mean a very special meal, a feast perhaps, or it can be part of a meal.

Antipasto can be as simple as you please, or as elaborate and decorative as your time, energy, and interest permit. The number of foods in antipasto made at home can range all the way from five to sixty varieties of meats, fish, chicken, eggs, vegetables, fruit, and combinations of foods such as salads and spreads, or a few simple vegetables, sprinkled with salt and dipped into a mixture of olive oil and freshly ground black pepper.

Foods included may be varied according to where you live, your own food traditions, the season of the year, the amount of money on hand, and your spirit of adventure in eating.

Start with your own food traditions. Adopt food traditions of other cultures that please you. By mixing or matching food traditions, you can create flavorful and attractive antipasto meals to suit your mood, whatever it may be. Here, for starters, are two delightful antipasto combinations.

Prosciutto Antipasto Meal

> Prosciutto, very thin slices
> Stuffed egg with anchovies
> Fresh finocchio (fennel)
> Chick peas, peppered to taste
> Pickled mushrooms
> Cherry tomatoes
> Bibb or Boston lettuce with blue cheese dressing

Complete the meal with crusty bread, spumoni, and something to drink.

Tips on Packing the Prosciutto Antipasto Meal

1. Pack salad greens, tomatoes, and finocchio in a plastic bag or bowl.
2. Pack the following in layers in a prechilled wide-mouth vacuum bottle in the following order:
   > Pickled mushrooms
   > Chick peas
   > Stuffed egg
   > Prosciutto slices, cut into small pieces or rolled to fit into bottle

   Cover at once.
3. Pack bread in a waxed paper bag or waxed paper. Stays crisp.
4. The spumoni (Italian ice cream) may be packed in a prechilled wide-mouth vacuum bottle. Spumoni must be hard when packed.
5. Pack salad dressing in small plastic container.

Soprassata/Mortadella Antipasto Meal

Mortadella, thin slices, or soprassata, thin
   slices (Italian pork sausage)
Fontina cheese, piece
Pimiento
Artichoke hearts, marinated
Radish roses
Olives
Eggplant relish
Watercress sprigs

Complete the meal with biscotto (hard, commercially
packaged twice-baked biscuits), fresh strawberries, plain,
or in white wine, with something to drink.

SPECIAL NOTE. A favorite Italian gourmet first
course is easy to serve. It's simply chilled cantaloupe or
honeydew melon wedges eaten with prosciutto, the Italian
ham. Another version is chilled fresh figs and prosciutto.

Scotch Eggs

Makes 6

1 pound well-seasoned sausage meat
1 egg, well beaten
¼ cup bread crumbs, approximately
6 hard-cooked eggs, shelled
   flour
   bread crumbs to coat eggs
   fat for deep-fat frying

Place well-seasoned sausage meat in a bowl. Add *half*
the well-beaten egg. Set aside the rest. Add ¼ cup bread
crumbs to sausage meat and egg. Mix well. If too wet to
form a ball, add a few additional teaspoons bread crumbs
and mix well. Divide into six equal portions. Set aside. Roll
shelled eggs in flour to coat. Shape each portion of sausage
mixture around egg until egg is covered as evenly as
possible. This may take a little time until meat is molded
to egg. Gently roll meat-covered egg in reserved beaten
egg. Then roll in bread crumbs. Allow to stand 5 minutes.

Fry in deep fat long enough to brown evenly and for the sausage meat to cook well. This should take about 10 to 15 minutes, depending on the thickness of the meat covering the egg. Cool. Pack in small plastic container or in a prechilled wide-mouth vacuum bottle as part of a layered cold meal.

Cioppino

Makes 4 to 6 servings

       2 tablespoons butter
       2 tablespoons olive oil
       1 medium-size onion, chopped
       1 clove garlic, finely minced
       1 small green pepper, finely chopped
      ½ cup thinly sliced celery
       4 large fresh tomatoes, peeled and cut into
             8 pieces
       1 cup tomato sauce or purée
      ⅓ cup dry sherry, if desired
       2 tablespoons tomato paste
       1 bay leaf
       1 teaspoon salt
       3 tablespoons finely chopped fresh parsley
      ½ teaspoon oregano
      ¼ teaspoon basil
          freshly ground black pepper
       1 pound large shrimp with tails, shelled and
             deveined
      ½ pound striped bass, haddock or cod fillets,
             cut into bite-size pieces
     12 bay scallops or 6 sea scallops, cut into
             12 pieces
     12 well-scrubbed little neck clams or mussels

Heat butter and oil in a large heavy Dutch oven or other heavy pot over medium heat. Add onion, garlic, green pepper, and celery. Sauté for about 5 minutes or until onion is transparent but not browned.

Stir in cut-up fresh tomatoes, tomato sauce or purée,

sherry, and tomato paste. Bring to boiling point. Cover. Turn down heat and simmer for 35 minutes. Stir occasionally. Should sauce cook down, add fish stock, clam juice, or a little water.

Stir in salt, parsley, oregano, and basil. Add bay leaf and freshly ground black pepper to taste. Cover. Simmer for an additional 25 minutes. Stir occasionally.

Arrange shelled shrimp, striped bass, and scallops in tomato sauce. Top with clams or mussels. Cover and cook over low heat for about 10 to 15 minutes or until clams are open and fish is done. Do not overcook. Cool and refrigerate until ready to use.

Spoon out a serving of cold cioppino into a saucepan, taking care to include some of the fish and each of the shell fish. Cover. Heat over medium low heat until hot. Remove clam or mussel shells and spoon cioppino into preheated wide-mouth vacuum bottle. Cover. Pack cioppino with a crusty French or Italian bread for lunch.

Green Salad with Caviar Dressing

> 1 to 1½ cups mixed salad greens per serving,
>   such as endive, arugula, red leaf
>   lettuce, romaine, etc.
> Caviar Dressing

Place a portion of the mixed greens on a plate or in a bowl. Spoon the amount of dressing wanted onto greens. Toss. Season to taste.

NOTE. Now is the time to use a pocket-size pepper mill, if you have been given this gift for the lunch box toter who has everything.

Caviar Dressing

Makes about 1 cup

> ½ cup mayonnaise
> ⅓ cup sour cream
> 1 ounce black caviar
> 1 tablespoon chili sauce, catsup, or bland
>   tomato sauce
> 1 teaspoon fresh lemon juice
>   onion juice to taste
>   salt to taste

Measure the mayonnaise, sour cream, caviar, chili sauce, lemon and onion juices into a bowl or refrigerator container. Stir until blended. Taste. If needed, add salt. Refrigerate until ready to use.

PACKING TIPS
1. Pack crisp greens in plastic bowl with cover or in a plastic bag.
2. Pack dressing in liquid-tight plastic container.

GOURMET SANDWICH SUGGESTIONS

Circular Sandwich

Pack in a plastic divided container small portions of caviar, egg salad, small squares of smoked salmon, watercress-cream cheese spread, and deviled ham. At lunchtime, place the caviar in the center of a round slice of pumpernickel bread. Instead of cutting a loaf of round pumpernickel bread vertically, cut it horizontally. In circular fashion, arrange first the egg salad around the caviar. Next, add a circle of smoked salmon, watercress-cream cheese spread, and deviled ham.

Country Ham Sandwich

Cut thin slices of whole wheat bread. Spread with egg butter spread or cheese butter spread. Top with paper-thin slices of cooked country ham. Pack in wrap or plastic sandwich container.

Lobster Salad Sandwich

Pack your favorite chilled lobster salad in a prechilled wide-mouth vacuum bottle or plastic container. At lunchtime spoon into a long, soft roll.

GOURMET INSULATOR SPREADS

Anchovy Butter

> ¼ cup sweet butter, softened
> 1 tablespoon mashed anchovies or
>   1½ teaspoons anchovy paste
> 1 tablespoon finely minced fresh parsley
>   few drops lemon juice
>   freshly ground black pepper to taste

Work butter with spoon until soft and creamy. Gradually work in with a spoon the anchovy and parsley. Add lemon juice and black pepper. Mix until well blended. Refrigerate overnight before using.

Egg Butter

> ¼ cup sweet butter
> 2 hard-cooked egg yolks, sieved
> 2 teaspoons finely minced chives
> 1 teaspoon finely minced celery
>   salt and freshly ground black pepper to taste

Work butter with a spoon until soft and creamy. Gradually work the sieved egg yolks in with a spoon until light and creamy. Add chives and celery. Mix until well blended. Add salt and pepper to taste. Blend until creamy. Refrigerate overnight before using.

Caviar Butter

¼ cup sweet butter, softened
2 tablespoons caviar
¼ teaspoon finely minced onion or chives
1 teaspoon lemon or lime juice

Work butter with spoon until soft and creamy. Gradually work the caviar and minced onion in with a spoon. Add lemon juice and mix well. Refrigerate overnight before using.

7 calorie-
controlled
tote meals

Lunch box toters can win the calorie game, and here are some effective ways to do it.

First, some background. Many people suffer creeping overweight. They gain a small amount each year, and pretty soon, they have a weight problem. This is reflected in the findings of the National Center for Health Statistics, a federal agency. They show that the average man surveyed from 1971 to 1974 weighed four pounds more than he did in a similar survey conducted a decade earlier. The average woman gained one pound. When the figures in the survey are compared with the Desirable Weights Guide of the Metropolitan Life Insurance Company, the projected figures show the average American man is twenty to thirty pounds overweight, and the average American woman is fifteen to thirty pounds overweight.

When people are overweight, it is usually related to overeating and underexercising. The solution is simple. Eat less, while increasing physical activity. This is easier said than done, but it's true that most people who have tried to lose weight by diet alone have failed. They need a realistic exercise plan as well as a diet.

Lunch toters can lose ten pounds a year merely by walking a brisk *additional* mile each day of the year during lunch hour, even if their lunches and other physical activity remain the same. For the toter who will eat one hundred calories less at lunch each day, another ten pounds will be lost at the end of the year. For example, when you cut out just one level tablespoon of mayonnaise, butter, or margarine from a tote lunch each day in the year, you will lose ten pounds at the end of the year. The same thing is true if each day you cut out ten potato chips, or two chocolate chip cookies, or two butter thin cookies, or an eight-ounce cola-type drink, or two tablespoons of deviled meat spread, or a quarter-pint of ice milk.

For those who want to lose weight more rapidly, follow the calorie-controlled lunch box meals given below. If you want to cut out even more calories, ways are given after each lunch box meal.

425-Calorie-Controlled Swiss Cheese Sandwich Tote Meal

Swiss Cheese Sandwich
Raw Mushroom and Spinach Salad
Tomato-Vinegar Dressing
Orange
Coffee or Tea

Calorie Breakdown

SANDWICH

2	slices whole wheat bread (18 slices per pound)	120 calories
1	tablespoon butter, margarine, or mayonnaise	100 calories
1	ounce slice Swiss cheese	105 calories

SALAD

1	cup chopped spinach, plus	15 calories
½	cup sliced raw mushrooms	10 calories

DRESSING

2	ounces tomato juice, plus	10 calories
1 to 2	teaspoons vinegar	0 calories
	sprinkle oregano	0 calories
1	orange (2⅝ inches in diameter)	65 calories
		425 calories

HOW TO REDUCE THE CALORIES. For those who want to or need to lose weight faster, this is how to reduce the 425-Calorie-Controlled Swiss Cheese Sandwich Tote Meal to 270 calories:

1. Change the sandwich to an open-faced Swiss cheese sandwich made with 1 slice of bread rather than 2 slices. A saving of 60 calories.
2. Instead of butter, spread the bread with 1 level tablespoon of mustard, using only 5 calories. A saving of 95 calories.

HOW TO PACK
1. Pack sandwich in wrap of your choice or in plastic sandwich container.
2. If mustard is used, pack in small plastic or other type container.
3. Pack greens and whole mushrooms in plastic bag or container. Slice mushrooms just before eating lunch.
4. Pack orange as is, or in wrap of your choice.
5. Pack coffee or tea in preheated regular vacuum bottle.

380-Calorie-Controlled Fruited Yogurt Tote Meal

Fruited Yogurt
Bran Muffin
Coffee or Tea

Calorie Breakdown

plain yogurt (8-ounce container) combined with	145 calories
½ sliced banana, 8¾ inches long	50 calories
½ apple with skin, chopped, 2¾-inch diameter	40 calories
½ sliced fresh peach	40 calories
bran muffin (2⅜-inch diameter, 1½ inches high)	105 calories
tea or coffee	0 calories
	380 calories

TO REDUCE TO 340 CALORIES. In place of bran muffin, substitute 1 slice raisin bread (18 slices to a loaf, or 3¾ inches wide, 3⅝ inches high, ½-inch thick). A saving of 40 calories.

Fruited Yogurt

> ½ sliced banana
> ½ apple with skin, chopped
> ½ peach, sliced
> 8 ounce container plain yogurt
> orange juice, 1 to 2 tablespoons

Place sliced banana, chopped apple, and sliced peach in a small bowl with tight-fitting cover. Add 1 to 2 tablespoons orange juice. Toss fruit gently so orange juice coats fruit. Gently stir in yogurt. Refrigerate until ready to pack lunch.

HOW TO PACK
1. Carry in bowl with tight-fitting cover or pack in prechilled wide-mouth vacuum bottle.
2. Pack muffin in wrap or bag of your choice.
3. Pack coffee or tea in preheated regular vacuum bottle.

280-Calorie-Controlled Camembert Finger Food Tote Lunch

Camembert Cheese
Pumpernickel Bread
Tomato Wedges and Watercress Sprigs
Fresh Apricots

Calorie Breakdown

1 wedge (1⅓ ounces) Camembert, cut into 3 pieces	115 calories
1 slice pumpernickel (5 x 4 x ⅜-inch thick) (about 14 slices to a pound) cut into 3 pieces	80 calories
1 tomato (2⅗-inch diameter) cut into wedges	25 calories
5 sprigs watercress	5 calories
3 fresh apricots, about 12 per pound	55 calories
coffee or tea	0 calories
	280 calories

HOW TO PACK
1. Pack cheese in wrap of your choice.
2. Pack bread in wrap of your choice.
3. Wrap tomato and watercress in plastic wrap or in container.
4. Pack apricots in wrap or plastic bag.
5. Pack hot coffee or tea in preheated vacuum bottle or if beverage is cold in precooled vacuum bottle.

265-Calorie-Controlled Salad Meal

Shrimp Cocktail on
Mixed Green Salad with Chili Sauce Dressing
Bread Sticks
Grapefruit
Tea, Coffee, or Milk

Calorie Breakdown

5 large, boiled shrimp, cooked	35 calories
DRESSING	
2 tablespoons chili sauce mixed	30 calories
with horseradish or lemon juice to taste	5 calories
1½ cups mixed green salad of watercress, romaine, and Boston lettuce	15 calories
2 plain bread sticks (7¾ inches long, ¾-inch diameter)	40 calories
½ grapefruit	50 calories
1 cup skim milk	90 calories
tea or coffee	0 calories
	265 calories

HOW TO PACK
1. Pack cold shrimp in container or prechilled wide-mouth vacuum bottle.
2. Pack dressing in small airtight plastic or other type container.
3. Pack mixed green salad in plastic bag or container.
4. Pack bread sticks in bag or wrap.
5. Pack grapefruit in plastic bag.
6. Pack milk and/or coffee in prechilled or preheated vacuum bottle.

275-Calorie-Controlled Soup Tote Meal

Chicken Egg Drop Soup
Carrot Sticks and Pepper Rings
Cantaloupe
Skim Milk
Coffee or Tea

Calorie Breakdown

1 cup fat-free clear chicken broth	0 calories
1 egg	80 calories
1 teaspoon grated Parmesan cheese	10 calories
parsley	0 calories
carrot sticks—5 strips	10 calories
pepper rings (1/3 pepper)	5 calories
cantaloupe (1/2 of 5-inch melon)	80 calories
skim milk, 1 cup	90 calories
coffee or tea	0 calories
	275 calories

Chicken Egg Drop Soup

Makes 1 serving

1 cup fat-free chicken broth
1 egg
1 teaspoon grated Parmesan cheese
1/2 teaspoon chopped parsley
salt and pepper to taste

Pour chicken broth into small saucepan. Heat to a rolling boil. Add, tablespoon at a time, mixture of well-beaten egg, cheese, parsley, salt, and pepper. Reduce heat and simmer until egg mixture puffs and is cooked. Pour hot soup into a preheated wide-mouth vacuum bottle.

HOW TO PACK

1. Pack soup in preheated wide-mouth vacuum bottle.
2. Pack carrots and pepper in moisture-proof wrap or container.
3. Pack cantaloupe in moisture-proof wrap or container.
4. Pack milk and/or tea or coffee in precooled or preheated vacuum bottle.

COTTAGE CHEESE COMBINATION TOTE MEALS

280-Calorie-Controlled Cottage Cheese Combination

Cottage Cheese Apple/Banana/Orange Combination
Mixed Greens
Blueberry Muffin
Coffee or Tea

Calorie Breakdown

¼ cup creamed cottage cheese	55 calories
½ chopped apple (2½-inch diameter, 4 to a pound)	30 calories
½ sliced small banana (7¾ inches long)	40 calories
½ sliced orange (2⅝-inch diameter)	35 calories
1 cup shredded salad greens such as romaine and escarole	10 calories
1 blueberry muffin (2⅜-inch diameter)	110 calories
coffee or tea	0 calories
	280 calories

310-Calorie-Controlled Cottage Cheese Combination

Cottage Cheese/Blue Cheese/
Tomato/Celery Combination
Mixed Greens such as
Chicory and Escarole
Bran Muffin
Coffee or Tea

Calorie Breakdown

½	ounce blue cheese	50 calories
½	cup cottage cheese	110 calories
1	chopped tomato (2⅗-inch diameter)	25 calories
½	cup chopped celery	10 calories
½	cup shredded chicory	5 calories
½	cup shredded escarole	5 calories
1	bran muffin (2⅜-inch diameter, 1½ inches high)	105 calories
	coffee or tea	0 calories
		310 calories

HOW TO PACK COTTAGE CHEESE COMBINATION
TOTE MEALS
1. Pack cottage cheese mixture in container or
   prechilled wide-mouth vacuum bottle.
2. Pack greens in moisture-proof container, plastic bag, or wrap.

400-Calorie-Controlled Cottage Cheese Combination

Cottage Cheese/Carrot/Green Pepper Combination
Watercress and Boston Lettuce Salad
Blue Cheese-Tomato Dressing
Corn Muffin
Banana
Coffee or Tea

Calorie Breakdown

½ cup creamed cottage cheese	110 calories	
¼ cup grated carrot	10 calories	
⅓ pod chopped green pepper	5 calories	
½ cup shredded watercress	5 calories	
½ cup shredded Boston lettuce	5 calories	

DRESSING

2 tablespoons tomato juice	10 calories
½ ounce blue cheese	50 calories
1 corn muffin (2¾-inch diameter and 1½ inches high)	125 calories
1 small banana	80 calories
coffee or tea	0 calories
	400 calories

---

3. Pack muffin in bag or wrap.
4. Pack coffee or tea in regular vacuum bottle. Precool bottle for cold drinks or preheat for hot drinks.
5. When a piece of fruit is included in lunch, pack as desired.

is it_____
enough
nutrition?

A good lunch includes:

1. **A Protein Food**
   Such as fish, cheese, eggs, meats, and poultry; peanut butter, dried beans, or peas in combination with milk or other complete protein food.

2. **A Vegetable High in Vitamin A or C, or Both**
   Examples of vegetables high in vitamin A are carrots, very dark green leafy vegetables, and salad greens. An example of a vegetable high in vitamin C is broccoli.

3. **Fruits High in Vitamin A and Vitamin C**
   An example of fruit high in vitamin C is the citrus group such as oranges and grapefruit. Strawberries are also high in vitamin C. An example of a fruit high in vitamin A is cantaloupe.

4. **A Cereal Food such as Enriched or Whole Grain Bread for B Vitamins and Iron**
   Include a whole grain bread as often as possible because it provides an important and inexpensive source of the B vitamins and iron, as well as bulk, or fiber.

5. **A Calcium-Rich Food such as Milk or Cheese**
   These foods also provide protein as well as riboflavin.

sanitation _____
and
health

The United States Department of Agriculture refers to the "brown bag blues," which is their term for food poisoning in connection with brown bagging it. The brown bag blues are accompanied by severe headache, diarrhea, vomiting, abdominal cramps, and fever after eating. These symptoms are often mistaken for flu or other stomach disturbances, but the brown bagger should first check them out for food poisoning, and see a doctor.

It's very easy to avoid these unpleasant symptoms of improperly prepared and packed food. The first rule is to prepare food for brown bagging in the same careful way as for meals eaten at home. It goes without saying that all the utensils, work areas, and the hands, should be scrupulously clean. To maintain surfaces in good order, scrub them before and after each use with a solution of bleach and water, according to the manufacturer's directions on the bleach container.

When handling raw meats or other raw foods, the hands should be thoroughly washed with soap and water before touching other foods, as there are food bacteria that can contaminate foods from such handling.

Hot food should be cooked thoroughly, and raw foods such as salad greens and fruits should be washed thoroughly with water.

When hot foods are packed in preheated vacuum bottles, it is important that the bottles be sanitized. You may

117

either follow the recommendations of the manufacturer of the vacuum bottle, or follow these directions. Wash the vacuum bottle with a mild detergent and very warm to hot water. Once the bottle is washed, pour in boiling water, cover for a few minutes, pour the water out and rinse the bottle thoroughly. It is a good idea to freshen the bottle periodically by adding a spoonful or two of baking soda and hot water. It is also important that vacuum bottles be stored uncovered, without their tops, cup or container.

Foods that spoil quickly are best packed in prechilled or preheated vacuum bottles. However, if you do not use these, you may pack the food in containers, chill the food, and use a thermo-insulated food carrier. Food should be treated and stored exactly the way you would treat it for lunch at home. Don't let the lunch stand at room temperature for long periods of time. Ignoring simple food care and personal hygiene can often mean the brown bag blues.

Concerning milk, if you do not have vacuum bottles, it is best to buy the milk at your place of work or school, just before you are ready to eat.

When packing hot or cold foods in a vacuum bottle, pack only just before you are ready to leave home. You cannot pack hot or cold food in a vacuum bottle the night before; it won't keep. Let the food stand in the refrigerator until you are ready to pack it.

If there is a refrigerator at work, refrigerate your lunch as soon as you arrive. Another way of keeping the lunch at the proper temperature to avoid food poisoning is by using a freezer-gel device, or make your own by freezing water in a liquid-tight plastic container and placing it in the lunch bag or box.

mini-catalog
of
lunch box
equipment

VACUUM BOTTLES

Standard-Neck Vacuum Bottle

SELECTION. A narrow or standard-neck vacuum bottle for carrying and keeping hot or cold clear liquids such as milk, coffee, tea, juices, etc. Various colors and designs from simple to sophisticated (photo).

SIZES. Half-pint, pint, quart sizes.

CONSTRUCTION. Available with plastic, stainless steel, steel, or aluminum outer case. In some premium-priced models, both the outer case and inner liner are made of stainless steel (see illustration 1). These offer the advantage of high durability and are ideal for carrying in trucks, long distances by car, camping trips, and anywhere bottles receive rough handling.

Most vacuum bottles are lined with glass vacuum insulation (see illustration 2). Because of this, they must be handled gently. We strongly advise that vacuum bottles to be used by children contain no glass lining (see illustration 3). You will find nonbreakable vacuum bottles that are urethane-insulated rather than glass-lined. These bottles have either a wide-mouthed top, which permits eating directly from the container or a narrow neck, for liquid only. Standard-neck vacuum bottles are available with or without handles. Some are designed to be mounted either in an office, car, or truck. A special vacuum caddy is available for dispensing coffee at the flick of a button (see illustration 4). There are also large-size vacuum bottles with pouring spouts that dispense hot or cold liquids when pressed at the top.

CARE. Vacuum bottles, like any other utensils used for storing or preparing food, should be thoroughly washed and sanitized. Bottles that have glass vacuum-insulated

1. *Thermos® Brand Standard Neck Vacuum Bottle*

2. *Aladdin's Stanley® Stainless Steel Vacuum Bottle*

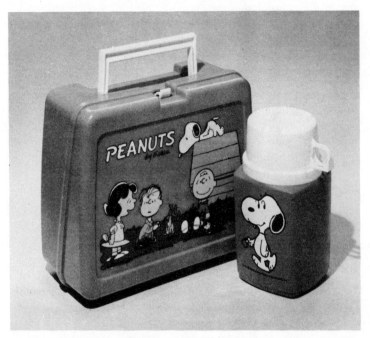

3. Thermos® Brand School Lunch Kit

fillers, need special care. This bottle may break if dropped, or shatter if the inside is struck with a hard object, such as a metal spoon, or if subjected to sudden extreme changes of temperature when filled. They require special care. If the bottles are stored in an unheated area such as a porch, or left in an automobile, it is best to rinse the bottle with cold tap water first, then wash with warm water and a mild detergent. Rinse with warm water, fill with warm-to-hot water, and let stand for a few minutes. After this process, to sanitize the bottle, add very hot water, and allow to stand with stopper on bottle for a few minutes. Pour out the water, place vacuum bottle in the dish drainer upside down and allow to air dry. The stopper and cup should be washed in sudsy water, rinsed thoroughly and dried. Should the vacuum bottle develop an odor, add 2 teaspoons of baking soda dissolved in very warm water. Allow this to stand in vacuum bottle for 20

Uno-Vac® Despens a Drink Vacuum Bottle Caddy

minutes, pour out, wash and rinse thoroughly. The baking soda freshens the bottle.

Never clean the bottle by immersing it completely in water, because in some bottles the water will penetrate the outer case. Bottles may be cleaned easily by filling them half-full with warm-to-hot sudsy water, screwing on the stopper, and shaking the bottle briskly. Adding a paper towel along with the water also helps clean the bottle. Rinse thoroughly. Never wash vacuum bottles in the dishwasher. All vacuum bottles should be stored uncovered after cleaning. Roll up a paper towel and stand it in the air-dried bottle to help absorb excess moisture. There may be exceptions in the way of cleaning such as with some stainless steel vacuum bottles. In these instances, simply follow manufacturer's directions.

SAFETY TIPS. Safety tips for glass vacuum-insulated bottles.

Carbonated beverages should never be carried in a vacuum bottle because the pressure created by the gases used in carbonation may cause leakage or shattering of the glass.

Never drink directly from any narrow-neck bottle.

Never add or carry ice cubes in it.

We strongly recommend that in opening a vacuum bottle with glass vacuum-insulated filler, the mouth of the bottle should be pointed away from anything that could be injured by broken glass. Unfortunately, in opening a bottle in which the glass has broken, there is the possibility that glass particles may come out of the mouth of the bottle as the stopper is removed. If you suspect that the filler has been broken, never drink the contents. Under most circumstances, the sound of broken glass will be audible.

WHERE TO BUY. Vacuum bottles may be purchased in variety, department, and hardware stores, national chains such as Sears, Montgomery Ward, J. C. Penney, sporting goods outlets, supermarkets, and other food stores, and in some areas, in drugstores. They are also available through direct mail catalogs.

Wide-Mouth Vacuum Bottles

SELECTION. Available in assorted colors and designs, and in the materials found in standard-neck bottles (see illustration 5). The wide-mouth vacuum bottle allows for carrying both hot and cold solid and semisolid foods such as hot main dishes, soups with vegetables, meats, and main dish salads.

SIZES. 10 ounces, pint, quart.

5. *Thermos® Brand Wide Mouth Vacuum Bottles*

CONSTRUCTION. Similar to that of standard-neck vacuum bottles except that most wide-mouth vacuum bottles are lined with plastic liners to protect the glass interior.

CARE. Same as above.

USE. To get the best use from a wide-mouth vacuum bottle, it should be either prechilled or preheated. For hot solid or semisolid foods, pour warm-to-hot water into a bottle that has reached room temperature. Cover and allow to stand for 5 minutes. Pour out the water and fill with the hot food to about an inch from the top. Screw on stopper. For cold foods, pour very cold water into vacuum bottle for a few minutes and allow to stand. Empty, and fill with cold food to within an inch of the top. You may also prechill vacuum bottles by placing them, uncovered, along with stopper in the refrigerator for 15 minutes. The wide-mouth vacuum bottle may be used to pack ice cream. The uncovered bottle should be placed empty in the refrigerator overnight. The stopper (not cup) should also be placed in the refrigerator or freezer. Just before leaving home, fill chilled bottle with *very* hard ice cream. Cover with chilled stopper immediately. We have found this keeps ice cream for about 4 hours. Avoid keeping bottle near radiators or sunlight.

A prechilled quart-size wide-mouth vacuum bottle with protective liner is the perfect carrier for a chilled baby's bottle.

SAFETY TIP. Never use ice cubes in glass vacuum-insulated bottles. However, when chilled liquids are carried in a wide-mouth vacuum bottle that is protected by an inner shield, ice cubes may be carried without damaging the bottle. It is safe to eat from wide-mouth vacuum bottles that are lined with a safety liner or shield. However, for those that are not so lined, we recommend that the food be transferred to the cup of the bottle for eating.

THERMO OR SNACK JARS

SELECTION. Various colors and designs.

SIZES. Standard 6 ounces or 10 ounces.

CONSTRUCTION. They are made in two ways. Some jars come with a plain top while others have tops that

*6. Aladdin's Insulated
    Thermo Jar*

are filled with pure distilled water; the tops can be placed in the freezer or ice cube compartment and will act as a miniature icebox whenever used for carrying in the snack or thermo jars. The best way to prechill the snack or thermo jar is to place the top and the jar, separately, uncovered, in the freezer (see photo).

USE. For puddings, coleslaw, potato salad, fruited salads, applesauce, cottage cheese, etc. Primarily used for chilled foods.

CARE. Wash in soapy, very warm to hot water, rinse and dry. Do not wash in electric dishwasher. Store uncovered. If used daily, store in freezer.

LUNCH BOX KITS

SELECTION. The range of lunch box kits varies from steel, plastic, and aluminum to tote bags of leatherlike material or fabric or thermo-insulated material. Lunch box kits may be equipped with assorted vacuum bottles as well as sandwich boxes. There are also foam-insulated lunch kits.

For instance, there is a workman-type lunch kit in plastic or metal with either a wide-mouth or standard-neck bottle. There are also kits in leatherlike shoulder tote style with one or two quart-size vacuum bottles and a sandwich box. Some kits are equipped with stainless steel bottles or bottles with glass insulation. There are everyday kits designed specifically for working women that include a pint-size vacuum bottle as well as space for the rest of the lunch.

For children, there are both plastic and metal kits with unbreakable vacuum bottles. Some are tote-bag style.

Other Lunch Boxes

Most of the lunch boxes above are also available without the vacuum bottles and/or sandwich boxes. In addi-

7. Nappe-Smith Thermo-Keep® Insulated Bags

tion, you will find a variety of thermo-insulated bags that keep food cold and safe. These bags range from cylinder shape to boxlike shapes that resemble a beach bag. One company makes a thermo bag with two smaller bags inside the large one. In this way, the cold foods stay cold while those to be kept hot stay hot. The sizes of the insulated bags vary to accommodate the needs of the toter on up to those bags that carry two vacuum bottles. For best results, follow directions provided by manufacturers.

Many people are carrying lunch in knapsnacks, which range from small to large. It is wise to purchase a waterproof knapsack if planning to use it to carry lunch.

Don't forget the always available brown paper bag, or a fabric or plastic tote bag, which you may have on hand.

For some people, the executive attaché case, if wide enough to hold a vacuum bottle, becomes the lunch box! So don't limit yourself. Look around and adopt your own style.

LUNCH BOX CARE. Wash with a mild detergent. Rinse. Dry. Leave open to ventilate when not in use.

Plastic Containers

SELECTION. Wide variety of designs, shapes, and sizes. Plastic ware with a leakproof tight-fitting cover or lid may be used for salads, salad dressings, sandwiches mixed dishes such as fruit cup, puddings, desserts, frozen juices, antipasto-type meals, midmorning snacks, salt and pepper or other condiments.

The plastic products used in the lunch box should be of good quality as well as sturdy because lunch boxes may be jostled or used roughly on a school bus, in a car, on a subway, etc. Here are some of the plastic items that we have found extremely helpful in packing our own lunches.

The plastic sandwich containers, a sandwich-size box with a tight-fitting cover. This container guarantees that the sandwich does not become mashed.

Individual side salad container with tight-fitting cover. This not only helps keep the salad crisp but ensures that it does not become crushed. These containers may also be used for main dish salads, fruit cup, some desserts,

8. Tupperware® Containers

etc. Some of the plastic containers for this use are constructed so that the cover on the container may be used as a plate.

Small plastic containers with tight-fitting lids that hold 2 ounces are excellent for salad dressings, salt, pepper, or sandwich spread; for those who eat dessert, they are great for fruit toppings for ice cream, or for pudding.

Plastic salt and pepper shakers. Look for salt and pepper shakers with hinged tops to prevent the contents from coming out. Many toters carry these daily. However, some toters keep them in a lunch box reserve place where they work.

Which type plastic ware one chooses depends upon the size of the lunch carrier. When the rectangular plastic container suits best the shape of your lunch box, use it for salads, both main dish and side salads, desserts, rolls, etc.

When you want to carry fragile fruit separtely, the 4½ ounce snack-size plastic container allows for carrying two or more fruits to be mixed in a salad. These also may be used for sliced pickles, olives, etc.

The half-cup capacity plastic sauce dishes and covers are excellent for carrying relishes, cranberry sauce, and a sandwich filling to be added to a partially packed sandwich.

When carrying salad for more than one person, use plastic salad bowls with liquid-tight covers in the 1- or 2-quart size. Many toters keep a bowl at work for mixing salads at lunchtime.

Tumblers, either of the 12-, 8- or 6-ounce size, with liquid-tight covers are excellent as refrigeration aids in the lunch box. Fill the tumbler with your favorite juice, leaving enough room at the top for expansion in freezing, cover properly and freeze. When the tumbler of frozen juice is packed with the lunch, it provides enough refrigeration to keep the rest of the meal cool until lunch hour.

Antipasto meals for one are easily packed in a plastic container that has three sections and a tight-fitting lid. In addition, the sectioned plastic container can be used to carry a main dish salad, a mixed green salad, and finger

9. Tupperware® Containers

sandwiches in one container. For those who entertain at lunchtime, there is a larger plastic container with six sections, in addition to a center area that would hold relish or olives. This type of container could carry enough food for two to four people, depending on the kind of meal packed.

Plastic lunch box. There is a lunch box that contains a sandwich box, a snack or dessert plastic container, a plastic tumbler with cover, and a square box with cover. This lunch box lends itself to a meal such as a sandwich, mixed green salad, pudding, and frozen juice. All the individual containers fit perfectly into the lunch box for compact carrying. The cover converts to a plate, if one does not want to eat from the containers. There is a removeable handle that has a space for an identification label. This type of box is ideal for the person who can buy milk or another beverage at work. It is excellent for children because it is light, there is nothing to break, and the milk can be purchased at school.

CARE. We do not recommend that plastic products be washed in an electric dishwasher because of the difference in water and drying cycle temperatures. Plastic products should be washed in sudsy water, as you would the family dishes. They should be dried and stored without the covers on, so that air can circulate in them. The covers should be stored flat so that the seal edge on the container is not affected. When covers of plastic containers are used as plates, be careful not to cut or puncture with a sharp knife. The same care should be taken not to puncture or cut into containers or edges of containers.

Do not use a plastic container to heat food if there is a microwave oven at your place of work. Instead, carry the food in the plastic containers and transfer the food to an appropriate plate to heat in the oven.

When plastic containers are to be used for freezing, be sure that the container you use is made for that purpose. Some plastic containers that are not meant for freezing will crack when frozen.

WHERE TO BUY. Plastic products are found usually in the housewares section of variety, department, and hard-

10. Tupperware® Lunch Box

ware stores. In addition, they may be found in grocery stores and in catalogs by direct mail. We have found the quality and variety of items is highest in the Tupperware plastic products, and they are the most popular with the toters we know. These products are not sold in stores but may be obtained usually by phoning the Tupperware distributor listed in the white pages of the local telephone directory under the name of Tupperware Home Parties. Toters have reported to us that some telephone books do not have this listing. In that case, write to Tupperware, Customer Relations Dept., P.O. Box 2353, Orlando, Florida 32802.

Some of the other companies that make a limited variety of high-quality items such as those described above are Rubbermaid, Republic Molding, Family Products, Inc., to name a few. You may also find a limited variety of plastic products for lunch box use through catalog companies such as Sears, J. C. Penney, Montgomery Ward, etc.

Recycled Containers

With the large number of containers used in packing foods such as margarine, cheese spreads, baby foods, jams, jellies, pickles, etc., the lunch box packer may want to take advantage of this bounty when the containers are liquid-tight and sturdy enough to fit lunch box needs. In addition, if the plastic bags in which fruits and vegetables are packed are washed, there is no reason why they cannot be used for lunch box carrying. One word of caution: If you decide to use glass containers, remember there is always the danger that they may break and cause a serious accident. For this reason, we recommend that glass containers never be used by children.

Plastic containers in which detergents are packed are a blessing to the person who works in an area where water is not available to wash one's hands. These containers can be filled with water for this purpose and discarded after use, or recycled.

Wraps or Bags

These are available in a number of materials. Which one you use depends on the cost, what the use is, and your own preference for a particular material.

Wraps come in waxed paper, plastic wrap, or aluminum foil. For sandwiches that are to be frozen, it is best to use freezer paper.

Bags come in plastic, waxed paper, as well as waxed coated papers, and brown paper.

Lunch Box Refrigerant

Use a freezer-gel device, which is usually sold in the same places where lunch box equipment is sold. The device is placed in the freezer or refrigerator compartment and enclosed in the lunch box or lunch bag. It is reusable and it keeps the lunch cold until you are ready to eat.

____index

5-879